Past-into-Present Series

WOMEN

Katharine Moore

B. T. BATSFORD LTD   London

396

First published 1970
© Katharine Moore 1970

Filmset by Keyspools Ltd., Golborne, Lancashire

Printed in Great Britain by Billing & Son Ltd, Guildford, Surrey
for the publishers
B. T. Batsford Ltd, 4 Fitzhardinge Street, London, W1.

7134 1760 9

Contents

Acknowledgment

The Author and Publishers wish to thank the following for permission to reproduce the illustrations included in this book: Ashmolean Museum for figs. 10, 35 and 42; Bodleian Library for figs. 6, 7 and 8; Trustees of the British Museum for figs. 2, 4 and 9; Central Press Photos Ltd for figs. 50 and 67; Fox Photos for fig. 66; Girton College Library for figs. 45 and 48; Imperial War Museum for fig. 64; A. F. Kersting for fig. 14; Mansell Collection for figs. 11, 15, 17, 25, 30, 31, 33, 37, 41, 43, 47, and 51; National Monuments Record (Crown Copyright Reserved) for fig. 5; National Portrait Gallery for fig. 12; *Radio Times* Hulton Picture Library for figs. 18, 29, 44, 53, 55, 58, 61, 62, 63, and 65; Trustees of the Victoria and Albert Museum for figs. 22, 23 and 26; Westminster Public Library for fig. 56; Women's Institute for figs. 59 and 60, and for permission to quote the poem by C. Day Lewis on p. 77. The remaining illustrations are taken from the Publisher's collection.

The Illustrations

1 The Medieval Englishwoman

The Englishwoman of the Middle Ages was, like the language she spoke, the product of a mixture of influences. Both the Celts and the Anglo-Saxons had revered women. When the Celts made a treaty with Hannibal they declared that the Carthaginians should bring any complaints before their women, in whose wisdom they trusted, and the Anglo-Saxons worshipped many female deities and often left their women in full charge of their affairs when they went off to fight. Classical civilisation, on the other hand, was essentially masculine. The Roman matron was certainly important within the family, but the virtues which were admired in her were devotion to her husband and children. Under Roman law women had no independent existence. The Middle Ages knew little of Greek writers except through Latin translations, but the best-known was perhaps Aristotle, who had written 'Moral goodness is possible in every type of personage, even in a woman or a slave, though the one is perhaps an inferior and the other a wholly worthless being.'

The influence of Christianity—the Old and the New Testaments, the teaching of the early Fathers and the pronouncements of the Church—was also of very great importance. Christianity established the belief that women as well as men had souls and the status of women was certainly raised by the worship of the Virgin Mary and of the women Saints. On the other hand, it was universally believed that it was through Eve that sin first came into the world and that, though man had been created in God's image, woman was made from man's rib simply to be of use to him: 'Him for God only, she for God in him' as Milton wrote. St Paul, too, influenced by both Roman and Eastern ideas, upheld the subservience of women.

In addition, the early Fathers of the Church placed a very high value upon chastity as a virtue for both sexes. They looked upon marriage almost as a necessary evil and proclaimed it to be a less holy way of life than that of the monk or nun vowed to chastity. So women came to be regarded by the Church as potential threats to those men who wished to live the life best pleasing to God and they were exhorted to take the utmost care not to lead men astray. Chaucer's jolly Wyf of Bath says 'It is impossible that any Cleric should speak good of women unless it be of the Holy Saints.'

Yet the Church did sometimes intervene on behalf of women. It was an age of physical violence and wives were often subject to brutal treatment. An early Church council says 'A Christian husband is bound to chastise his wife *moderately*,' and in 1344 Parliament complained that 'the Church wished to allow serfs and

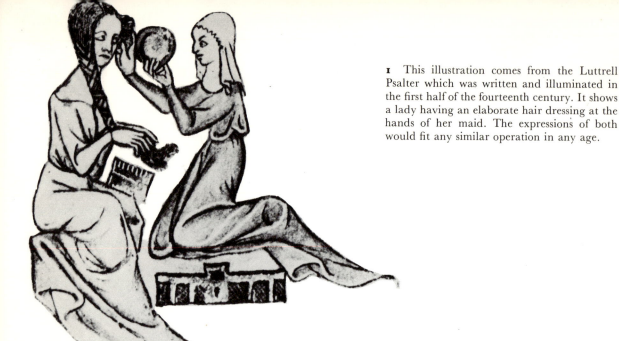

women to make wills, which is against reason.' The Church had its ideal pattern for Christian women which did not alter much through the ages—'She must be pure of countenance, neither her brow downcast nor her eyes uplifted, her head not poked forward, her limbs not lounging. Spinning and weaving, the making of garments, the care of the household, the preparation of food, these are the occupations which belong to God's law of life for a woman.'

There was yet another powerful influence on the ideas held about women in the Middle Ages. This was the romantic conception of the remote, and adored, lady-love for whom knights and squires rode forth to gain honour and renown. The poetry of the age is full of this visionary being and there is a reason for this. Marriage in those days was a bargain between parents for material gain. Child marriages were common. Much of the Church teaching on marriage was, as we have seen, mundane, so men sought for romantic love outside their marriage. The mere thought of everyday intimacy was distasteful and they preferred to worship from afar. This idealistic treatment of women was harmful, in that it was unrealistic, but perhaps it did help to make men gentler and more respectful to women in general.

These are the outstanding ideas which shaped the attitudes towards English-women in the Middle Ages and influenced their lives. Echoes of them persisted right through the centuries. But there is always plenty of difference between theory and practice. We know quite well that actual living women would never fit neatly into either the classical, clerical or chivalric pattern. Let us look at some of the contemporary portraits that have come down to us.

8

There were only two ways of life open to medieval gentlewomen—the life of a nun or a wife and there was little choice allowed about either. If a girl wished to enter a convent but her father required her to make an advantageous marriage, marry she must. If, on the other hand, the chances of a favourable marriage were not good, either through the hazards of war, or through some personal disability or for any other reason, into the convent the girl must go, though the thought of a life of prayer and poverty might be hateful to her. That this did not make for holiness became obvious as the convents grew more lax. The nuns tried to escape from the early rules of self-discipline and service.

Chaucer has left us a vivid picture of a Prioress of the fourteenth century who was one of his Canterbury pilgrims. She was a fine lady with very good manners. She could speak French, though not quite like a Frenchwoman, and could intone the Church services in the correct manner through her nose(!). Her cloak was worn with much grace and fastened with a brooch with the somewhat ambiguous motto 'Love conquers all'. She was very gentle and tender-hearted but she was not in the least holy. She kept pet dogs which she was not allowed to do, nor should she by rights be going on this pilgrimage at all. Yet everyone took her for granted.

Nearly a century earlier the Bishop of Salisbury had written in a book called *The Nun's Rule* 'wear no iron, nor haircloth, nor hedgehog skins; and do not

2 Chaucer's Prioress who by the rules of her order should have remained within her convent, is here pictured charmingly attired and riding on a graceful palfrey with ornamental harness. She is thoroughly enjoying her spring outing to visit the shrine of Thomas à Becket at Canterbury. She certainly had no vocation but had been placed in the convent as a girl by her father and had risen to the position of Prioress through the influence of her family and her own good manners and general ability. Her rule was not likely to be strict.

3 From the Middle Ages right up to the eighteenth century women were associated with the art of healing. The most famous medieval hospital in Britain was at the nunnery at Sion on Thames. The Guild of Surgeons in 1389 recognised women as members. Here we see a medieval woman practitioner mixing medicine in a large pot by the fire. She is reading instructions from the book on her lap. A maid servant stands by to assist and the patient, evidently a man of means, lies awaiting her ministrations.

beat yourselves therewith . . . and let your shoes be thick and warm'. This implies that earlier in this period there had been nuns who had had a true vocation and were even excessively pious. Though even the Bishop finds it necessary to add 'Have neither ring nor brooch, nor ornamental girdle, nor gloves, nor any such thing that is not proper for you to have. And ye shall not possess any beast, my dear sisters, except only a cat'. He would not have approved of Chaucer's Prioress.

For the portrait of a well-born medieval wife we turn to a collection of letters belonging to a noble Norfolk family called Paston. Margaret Paston, wife to Sir John in the mid-fifteenth century, led a busy and responsible life. She had to look after and order a large number of servants, to know all about both the curing and preserving, as well as the cooking, of fish and meat, for each household had to lay in a stock which would last them through the winter. She had, besides, to know a great deal about the use of all kinds of herbs and how to doctor her children and servants. Her husband had often to leave her, for these were troublesome times. Ultimately Sir John lost his life in the Wars of the Roses. It is reassuring to find that here was a couple who managed to love each other in spite of all the ideas and practices which made married love somewhat difficult to achieve. Margaret frets about her husband and vows to make a pilgrimage to pray for him when he was ill and writes that 'she would rather have him safe at home than a new gown, though it were of scarlett'. She does not hesitate to ask him to make all sorts of purchases for her in London—of wooden plates and sugar and almonds and some cloth to make the children clothes—none of these could she apparently get in Norwich. She also asks him for a necklace, saying that when Queen Margaret visited Norwich and she was summoned to Court, she had no jewels of her own to wear and had to borrow her cousin's beads.

A step or so lower in the social grade we have another wife who certainly does not conform to the pattern of lowly submission. Chaucer's Wyf of Bath had had five husbands and got the better of them all. The last one, in order to stop her gadding about, was reading one day to her from his favourite book that dealt with stories of wicked wives. This so infuriated her that she tore away the page. Whereupon

> *He started up and smote me on the head*
> *And down I fell upon the floor for dead.*

This was by no means an unusual habit of husbands but the Wife of Bath knew how to manage even this to her own advantage and finally

> *He gave the bridle over to my hand,*
> *Gave me the government of house and land,*
> *Of tongue and fist, indeed of all he'd got.*
> *I made him burn that book upon the spot.*

4 We can guess at the masterful character of the Wyf of Bath, in this early illustration, by the way she is grasping the reins and wielding the whip. She wears the usual dress of the medieval middle-class housewife but Chaucer tells us that everything was of fine quality for she was a thoroughly good business woman and could afford the best. She sits astride her horse (for she is not genteel like the Prioress, who uses a side saddle), and we are told she sits 'easily' for she was a most experienced traveller.

And off she went on her gay gadding all over England and Europe, though she was a little deaf all the rest of her life from that blow. Chaucer's characters are not only individuals but types and we may be sure that his 'Prioresse' and his 'Wyf of Bath' were not exceptional. Indeed, there are other contemporary portraits which are closely akin to the 'Wyf of Bath'. The writers of the old Miracle Plays imagined the Biblical characters as being like themselves and their neighbours; Mrs Noah and her friends, or gossips as she calls them, of the Chester Plays are full of a sturdy obstinacy and a sixteenth-century writer, Richard Hilles, has some verses about wives who met to feast together in spite of their husbands—

> *A stripe or two God might send me*
> *If my husband might here see me,*
> *She that is afeared, let her flee,*
> *Quoth Alice then—'I dread no men'.*

Yet, though rebel wives did exist and happy marriages too, like Margaret Paston's, there are also records of much suffering and injustice. Then, indeed in

5 Brass at St Peter's Church, Ketteringham, of medieval knight and lady with their family.

6 A medieval woman milking.

every age, the lot of the deserted wife was hard and although divorce as such was unknown before the Reformation, it was easy enough for a man to break up his marriage if he wished. There were intricate tables of relationships within which a marriage was not valid and from Henry VIII downwards it was common to juggle about with these and to get a marriage annulled by the Church. Bribery, too, was common. A satiric verse in the reign of Edward II says:

> If a man have a wyf
> And he love her nowt
> Bring her to the Court
> There truth should be wrought.
> Bring two false witnesses with him
> And himself the third
> And he shall be separated
> As quickly as he would wish
> From his wyf.

Such deserted women had no redress and no aid except perhaps from their own relatives. Widows were also often left destitute though, as again we learn from Chaucer, re-marriage, in those times of sudden early deaths, was common.

It is hard to find any records of the poor and humble. It is probable that they were less disqualified by their sex than their betters. They often shared the same work as their husbands and had greater freedom of choice in marriage as neither property nor influence would have entered into the matter. We may be sure, though, that their life was extremely hard. Indeed all women in medieval times seem to have worked hard. The wealthy had large households to rule; the

7, 8 Scything and reaping.

middle-classes were often good business women as was Chaucer's Wyf of Bath who had been in her time a famous clothmaker. In an old book of husbandry it says 'It is a wyves occupation to wynowe all manor of cornes, to make malte, to washe and wrynge, to make hay, shere corn and in tyme of nede to helpe her husbande to fyll the muck-wayne and dryve the plough'. She was also responsible for the garden and, when she could not be out-of-doors, to be busy at her spinning and weaving!

One thing the medieval girl did *not* have to spend much time over was book-learning. Girls of good family learnt reading and writing and those destined for the convent might be given a slightly better education within the convent walls. It was the custom for many little girls of good birth to be boarded out in the families of the nobility where they were taught a great deal of embroidery, some music, French and household management. But both books and leisure were scarce and we have to wait till the Renaissance and Reformation had done their work for any notable women scholars to emerge.

2   The Renaissance and Reformation

The sixteenth century was as revolutionary an age as our own. New knowledge poured into Europe through the re-discovery of Greek learning, and the invention of printing spread this rebirth of thought, or renaissance, everywhere. Then, partly as a result of this ferment, came the breakaway from the age-old domination of Rome which we call the Reformation. Both of these great movements affected the lives of women.

Plato, now studied first-hand by English scholars, advised that boys and girls should share the same education. Learned men such as Vives, tutor to Princess Mary (Tudor); Ascham, tutor to Princess Elizabeth; Erasmus and Sir Thomas More actually thought it worthwhile to discuss seriously the whole question of women's education. They wrote of them as though they were reasonable beings, able to contribute with intelligence to society and, by a happy chance, there seems to have been a group of exceptionally clever and industrious girls among the Tudor nobility who were both willing and able to become paragons of virtue

9 This beautiful portrait by Holbein is most probably of Margaret Roper, the favourite daughter of Sir Thomas More. It certainly shows a likeness to him and the clever sensitive face fits well with what we know of her character. She was one of the famous group of sixteenth-century girl scholars. She helped her husband write the life of her father.

10 Holbein's drawing of this middle-class Englishwoman shows something of the new life and vigour which flooded into the country after the Renaissance. She may well have belonged to the enlightened household of Sir Thomas More.

and learning. Or, perhaps, it was *not* chance but the natural result of the opportunity given, for the first time in history, to the daughters of clever men to prove their worth.

At any rate, the Princesses Mary and Elizabeth; Lady Jane Grey; Ann, the daughter of Protector Somerset; Frances Brandon, a grand-daughter of Henry VII; Lady Jane Howard, daughter of the Earl of Surrey; Lady Jane Fitzalan, daughter of the Earl of Arundel; Sir Thomas More's daughters and a number of others of similar birth and ability, devoted themselves to studies which included a thorough knowledge of Greek and Latin, Hebrew and modern languages, besides philosophy, astronomy, 'physic', arithmetic, logic, rhetoric, music and theology. Nicholas Udall, a friend of Erasmus, wrote to Catherine Parr of 'the great number of noble women at that time in England not only given to the study of humane sciences and strange tongues, but also so thoroughly expert in the Holy Scriptures that they were able to compare with the best writers . . . as also translating good books out of Latin and Greek into English . . . It is now no news in England to see young damsels in noble houses familiarly both to read and reason thereof in Greek, Latin, French or Italian'.

Margaret, Sir Thomas More's favourite daughter, was a particularly attractive example of these Tudor paragons. He tells her once, with pride, how he showed a letter of hers to Cardinal Pole. 'Why should I not report what he sayd unto me? So pure a stile, so good Latine, so eloquent, so full of sweete affections, he was marvellously ravished with it.'

Of another charming Tudor scholar the poet Ben Jonson wrote

> *Sidney's sister, Pembroke's mother,*
> *Death, ere thou hast slain another,*
> *Learn'd and fair and good as she*
> *Time shall throw a dart at thee.*

She filled her home 'with learned and ingenious persons. She was the greatest patronesse of wit and learning of any lady in her time. She was a great chymist and spent yearly a great deal in that study'. Plato's ruling that girls should share not only learning but gymnastics with boys was too much even for Renaissance humanists and though Erasmus does suggest the advisability of lighter clothing, it was generally thought that women would get enough exercise by going briskly about their household tasks.

Of course the opportunity for all this study was given to only a few, but the fact that those few proved, by their shining achievements, that women were capable of benefiting by such an opportunity had its effect upon society as a whole. That Elizabeth, the most brilliant of this group of noble scholars, became a powerful and beloved Queen emphasised the success of the experiment. The strange thing is that the lesson was completely ignored by future generations. The range of subjects taught and the depth in which they were studied during this period was not approached again until the twentieth century, except by the

Although I coulde not be plentiful in giuinge thankes for the manifolde kindenis receyu at your hithnis hande at my departure, yet I am some thinge to be borne with al, for truly I was replete with sorowe to departe frome your highnis, especially seuinge you vndoubful of helthe, and albeit I answered litel I wayed it more dipper whan you sayd you wolde warne me of al exelles that you shulde hire of me, for if your grace had not a good opinion of me you wolde not haue offered frindeship to me that way, that al men iuge the contrarye, but what may I more say, than thanke God for pro-uidinge suche frendes to me, desiringe God to enriche me with ther longe life, and me grace to be in hart no les thankeful to receyue it, than I nowe am glad in wri-tinge to shewe it. and althongth I haue plentye of matter, hire I wil staye for I knowe you ar not quiet to rede . Frome Cheston this present saterday .

Your hithnis humble doughte

Elizabeth

11 Part of a letter written by Queen Elizabeth, when a girl of 14, to her stepmother, Catherine Parr. She was an intelligent and learned woman and took a kindly interest in the lonely young princess who gratefully returned her affection as this letter shows. Queen Catherine encouraged her in her scholarly pursuits. She must have enjoyed receiving letters in such a beautiful and clear handwriting.

eighteenth-century bluestockings and then in the teeth of much opposition and contempt.

It was not only among the nobility that the idea of new opportunities for girls' education was current. Thomas Becon in Edward VI's reign wrote 'It is expedient that, by public authority schools for women children be erected in every Christian commonweal. If it be thought convenient that schools should be set up for the right education and bringing up of the youth of the male kind, why should it not also be thought convenient that schools be built for the virtuous bringing up of the youth of the female kind? Is not the woman the creature of God as well as the man? . . . Is not the woman a necessary member of the common-weal?' And in Elizabeth I's time, a schoolmaster, Richard Mulcaster, pleaded that girls should be taught for their own sakes and for the sake of society. 'She has been given the power to learn by God,' he concludes, 'and myself am for them tooth and nail.'

The closing of all convent schools made this a special need and a number of grammar schools, though not enough, were founded for girls as well as boys. Some were co-educational. The trouble often was that there were too few women teachers, though these in some degree were supplied by Protestant refugees from Europe, who taught the little girls weaving and lace-making and other crafts, as well as their books.

There was no conflict between piety and learning. The influence of the Reformation was on the whole favourable to women. In getting rid of monasticism and in allowing priests to marry, the reformed Church raised the status of marriage and the clergy's wives were allotted work and responsibility outside their families, which was a new experience for housewives. Some of the more fanatical Puritans, John Knox for instance, later preached against women for the same reasons as the early Fathers had done, but the tide of opinion was set against them. On women themselves the impact of the reformed Faith was even more powerful than the new learning. The governess of Princess Elizabeth Stuart (another royal scholar) wrote in the seventeenth century 'Our very Reformation of Religion seems to be begun and carried on by women,' and sincere enthusiasm for the study of the Bible and theology continued well into the seventeenth century. In all the political troubles which beset the royal scholars, ending for some of them in tragedy, and for others in the common lot of their humbler sisters, of

12 The family of Sir Thomas More, by unknown artist, 1593. Sir Thomas More's daughters were highly educated. Erasmus wrote to Margaret in 1529 on receipt of this portrait group: 'Holbein's picture showed me the whole dear family so expressively that if I had been among you in person I could hardly have observed you all better.'

sickness and pain and the all too frequent loss of children, the women of both the sixteenth and seventeenth centuries had a strong and lively faith to uphold them.

The growth in the importance of women in society is reflected in literature. Shakespeare, then it must be remembered a popular writer, the idol of undergraduates, can safely be taken as reflecting public opinion, and his women characters are the equals or superiors of the men in play after play. Portia, Rosalind, Beatrice, Viola, Imogen and Perdita are wise and witty. They are also capable and some of them are learned. Mention of girls' schools and teachers in the plays is not uncommon. Helena and Hermia went to school together and Baptista, in *The Taming of the Shrew*, is anxious to find a good tutor for his daughters —'one well read in poetry and other books and cunning in music and mathematics.'

We can trace the likeness between Shakespeare's heroines and the early paragons of the Renaissance and Reformation but, though still virtuous, they are much more light-hearted. Life in Elizabeth's reign had become easier for all but the very poor, and women had their share of the enjoyment of festivals and feasts and shows—some of them coarse enough—that were so popular. A great deal of money was spent on food and dress: a lady's court dress would cost about two to four thousand pounds of our currency. Laws were passed limiting the size of ruffs and farthingales (enormous skirts), but they could not be enforced. The demand for all sorts of articles of dress resulted in more work and prosperity for women generally. There is a pleasant description of Queen Elizabeth's special interest, while at Norwich, in part of a show put on for her entertainment. This consisted in a green bank 'whereon eight small women-children were weaving yarn and eight more knitting stockings' while a small boy recited:

We bought before the things, that now we sell,
These slender imps, their work does pass the waves,
God's peace and thine we hold and prosper well.

William Harrison, who has left us a contemporary account of late sixteenth-century England, tells how delight in dress, and especially in French fashions, spread from the Court over the whole country. He also remarks on the growth of luxuries, though we should call them necessities, chimneys, window-glass, feather beds and pillows (instead of straw pallets and wooden billets), fine linen, pewter plates and drinking vessels—all these were new. Elizabethan houses, too, were more comfortable than any which had been built before. The home and its equipment are always of great importance in the life of the housewife. Foreign travellers in England remarked on the great good fortune of Englishwomen compared with those of other countries at this time, and on the respect in which they were held.

The Tudor and early Jacobean periods, then, mark a great advance in the history of English women both in education, in the status of marriage and in the comforts of life generally, but the conflict between King and Parliament in the mid-seventeenth century was to bring this comparatively golden age to an end.

14 A Tudor manor house (at Bletchingley, Surrey) with enlarged windows and chimneys.

3   The Civil War and its Aftermath

A Civil war, which may set son against father, brother against brother or married daughters against their parents, brings particularly acute sorrow to women. There was also frequently the loss of home and fortune for those of the King's party. There were many heroic wives on both sides and some names have come down to us of those who helped their husbands with outstanding courage and devotion. Some of the first memoirs written by women date from this period. The Duchess of Newcastle and Lady Fanshawe for the Cavaliers, and Lucy Hutchinson, wife of a Cromwellian colonel, all wrote lives of their husbands, and there are other family records such as those of the Verneys, from which we can learn what was demanded and what was given by women during these difficult times. It is worth noting that these eminent women were the product of the greater freedom and better education of the preceding age. Their daughters often had little opportunity for such an upbringing.

Lucy Hutchinson 'dressed wounds as well as any man's surgeon' and insisted on treating Royalist prisoners as well as Puritan soldiers, and Lady Fanshawe's and Lady Mary Verney's stories are representative of the lives of many Royalist wives. There is little to choose between the piety and resourcefulness of either side but naturally there was more call for courage from the women whose husbands were imprisoned or exiled.

Lady Fanshawe's married life was a series of separations and hardships, of shipwrecks and escapes, of robberies, forged passports and disguises (on one occasion as a cabin boy), of missions to England alone to try and raise money and all carried out through constant pregnancies and illness. She was devoted to her husband and when he was imprisoned after the Battle of Worcester she writes 'I failed not constantly to go, when the clock struck four in the morning, with a dark lantern in my hand, all alone and on foot, from my lodging in Chancery Lane. There I would go under his window and softly call him: thus we talked together and sometimes I was so wet with the rain, that it went in at my neck and out at my heels.' On this occasion she saved Sir Richard Fanshawe's life as he became very ill and it was only after her constant soliciting that Cromwell released him.

Mary Verney accompanied her husband to France and spent her time teaching her two children, and sewing and baking for the whole household. At length she, too, went over to England alone to try and get back the family estates. She had to fight with Lords and Commons, to administer judicious bribes, pay debts and try to get debts repaid to her. She, too, was ill (a child was born while she was in

15 Lady Fanshawe, one of the most intrepid among the heroic wives of the Civil War.

the midst of all this business) and she was very anxious about the children she had left behind, not without cause, for they both died during her absence. She was successful, however, in her mission.

The patient courage and the capacity of these women and others like them are notable and so is the trust their husbands placed in them. They had led disciplined and responsible, yet enjoyable lives up to the outbreak of the troubles and when the time came they met the challenge admirably. We know much more about them than the women of an earlier date because this was the first great age of diaries and letter-writing. The spread of education among women and the frequent partings and insecurity brought about by the war encouraged this habit.

Some of the pleasantest letters were written by a girl called Dorothy Osborne to her future husband, Sir William Temple. Dorothy's family were Royalist and her brother once got the family into serious trouble with Cromwell's troops by writing Royalist slogans on the window of an inn with his diamond ring. The whole party was taken into custody but Dorothy took the blame on herself and so they were released. This story is interesting because it shows the respect paid to gentlewomen even by the soldiers of the enemy. It was on this occasion that William Temple, a young Parliamentarian, fell in love with Dorothy there and

then. As the families belonged to opposite parties the match was unpopular with both sets of parents and the lovers were kept apart for over two years. Just before the wedding Dorothy fell ill of the dreaded smallpox, especially feared by women as, even if it spared their lives, it seldom spared their looks. The fashion of wearing black patches on the face was started to hide the marks left by the illness. Smallpox made no difference, however, to this particular love match.

Dorothy's letters reveal that she was not a scholar though she knew some Italian and Latin, loved poetry and French romances and was interested in the new discoveries of science. She was obviously a normally intelligent girl with a gift for charming and sincere self-expression. She does not approve of eccentric women and writes of the Duchess of Newcastle that she must be a little mad 'or she could never be so ridiculous else as to venture at writing books and in verse too!' She was naturally keenly alive to the political issues of the day but dare not say much of them—'I shall talk treason by and by if I do not look to myself. Tis safer talking of the orange flower water you sent me.'

Dorothy kept house for her father and was pestered by suitors. She was attended by a lady companion. These companions for women of quality became very fashionable and Mrs Pepys asked her husband for one as a status symbol. They were generally unmarried women of good birth who were otherwise unprovided for. The war made husbands and dowries hard to come by; Sir Ralph Verney was left with five unmarried sisters on his hands and how to dispose of them was a problem. Luckily husbands turned up in time and the youngest, Betsy, at 29, took matters into her own hands and made a runaway match beneath her— 'I am not so much lost,' she writes to her brother 'as sum thinck I am, becos I have married one, as has the reput of an onerst man, and one, as in time I may live comfortably with.'

But for those less lucky the position of superior maid or companion was a solution. Dorothy Osborne's companion was useful to her in keeping off the unwelcome suitors pressed on her by her father and brother. However, she was *not* forced into an unwelcome marriage for though marriages were still often arranged, and though sometimes the girls were very young (Mary Verney was only 13 and Elizabeth Pepys 15) the feeling against coercion was strengthening. Physical ill-treatment was also less common. Pepys has the grace to be ashamed of himself when once, provoked by his pretty little wife he 'struck her such a blow as made the poor wretch cry out' and he seems to have admired her for trying to bite and scratch him in return. He was also concerned because the people of the house observed it!

17 The ordeal by water of Mary Sutton, from a pamphlet, 1613, entitled 'Witches apprehended, examined and executed'. The persecution of women reputed to be witches greatly increased with the growth of Puritanism in the seventeenth century (see p. 30).

The heroic mould of womanhood was temporarily exhausted by the Civil War and a new type emerged in the fashionable society of the Restoration. She was often a wit, but not after the model of Shakespeare's heroines. She was pleasure-loving to a degree never observed before and her morals were questionable. You can find many such characters in Restoration drama and it is noteworthy that, whereas under Charles I, people were scandalised at the Queen and her ladies taking part in Court masques, under his son they flocked to see women acting for the first time in the public theatres and expressing themselves with a licence not met with again till our own day. A seventeenth-century writer Mrs Makin laments that 'there is not only lack of learning but of virtue among women of good position.' Cards, dancing, dress and scandal seem to have been their chief pursuit. In Congreve's *Way of the World* the hero addresses his wife thus 'When you shall be Breeding . . . I denounce against all strait-lacing, squeezing for a shape, till you mold my Boy's Head like a sugar loaf [and beg] that you restrain

18 Music was an important part of a girl's education in the seventeenth century. Here is a lady in 1635 playing the clavier, a favourite domestic musical instrument, and the forerunner of the piano.

yourself to a genuine and authorised tea table talk—such as mending of Fashions, Spoiling Reputations, railing at absent Friends and so forth.'

The decline in morals and learning among women was partly the reaction from enforced puritanism, partly the inescapable neglect which the children of many of the leading families had suffered during the war. The perils and privations of one generation are seldom interesting to the next and there was a wide rift between the young, who followed the new fashions, and those who clung to a more serious way of life. A similar situation has followed the wars of the twentieth century. In 1674 Carey, one of the Verney sisters writes to her brother in distress about her step-daughter Ursula who 'after eight months pleasure [in town] came home unsatisfied and now hath been at all the Salisbury races.' She borrowed a coach to go to these and was reported as 'dancing like wild' with a Mr Clark of doubtful character. She apparently returned when the family was all in bed, with another man, a Mr Tourner 'I know him not but he was tried for his life last November for killing a man. She had never been in bed since she went away till 4, and danced some nights till seven. She, declaring she could not be pleased without dancing 12 hours in the 24 and taking it ill that I would not have 7 ranting fellows to come here and bring music, and was very angrey and we had a great quarrel.' The final straw was that she brought home all the undesirable Mr Tourner's linen to be washed!

Some women of a serious turn who were involved in public affairs led a difficult life. Such a one was Mrs Godolphin, the great friend of John Evelyn, who wrote her biography. She was a lady-in-waiting but went to her duties 'fortified by prayer' and determined 'not to talk foolishly to men: *more especially the King*' and never to join in when 'they are speaking of plays and laughing at devout People.' Others, like Lady Falkland, retired into the country and spent her time in good works 'with a book, a wheel, and a maid or two.'

Girls' education had become largely devoted to accomplishments even in the best schools, which were mainly boarding schools for the wealthy. Needlework, strawwork, waxwork and similar ornamental handicrafts were the chief subjects. Music and acting were popular. Purcell's famous *Dido and Aeneas* was written for a girl's school to perform, but girls often left school with a very insubstantial groundwork of knowledge. The spelling and writing of the Verney girls are of a poor standard. Samuel Pepys, to keep his wife from mischief, gave her lessons himself in arithmetic and geography. This near illiteracy bore hardest on the middle-class townswoman like Elizabeth Pepys; the farmer's wife may have been unable to read or write but she was thoroughly capable in all practical matters and kept exceedingly busy. Fuller's *Worthies* tell that 'the country housewife must proceed more from the provision of her own yard than the furniture of the market and nearly all her goods were baked or brewed, or cured or preserved, or spun or woven at home.' Thomas Tusser, in his *Good Husbandry* says:

> *Though husbandrie seemeth to bring in the gains*
> *Yet huswiferie labours seeme equal in panes.*

19, 20   A merchant's daughter and a countrywoman.

The farmer's wife's domain extended over her house, garden and poultry yard but she was not required to care for livestock, or work in the fields. Outdoor women servants were kept for this. Dorothy Osborne describes how she used to 'walk out in a common . . . where a great many young wenches keep sheep and cows, sitting in the shade singing of Ballads . . . I talke to them and finde they want nothing to make them the happiest people in the world but the knowledge that they are so.' Sir Thomas Overbury also writes in his *Characters* of 'a faire and happy milkmaid [whose] garden and bee hive are all her physick and chyrurgery and she lives the longer for it. She dares goe alone and unfold sheepe in the night and feares no manner of ill, because she means none; yet to say truth, she is never alone, for she is still accompanied with old songs, honest thoughts and prayers, but short ones.' These portraits are no doubt idealised, but a fair standard of industry and good behaviour was required by the farmer's wife, for the girls lived under her roof as part of the family.

Other paid occupations for the working woman were knitting, especially of the silk stockings that had come into fashion in Elizabeth's day, drapers, sempsters in all sorts of needlework, lace and button and pin makers and vintners, which last seems to have been a curious trade for women. To all these trades girls were apprenticed for periods of from eight to 16 years. There were quite high premiums paid and employers were bound to feed and clothe their apprentices and generally to give them some wage after the first year or two. There were safeguards provided against the girl being used as a domestic drudge and, when parents or friends were near and masters and mistresses honest and kind, the system often worked well. It had done best in Tudor times and was to deteriorate badly in the eighteenth century. Women's trades were always less well protected than men's and subject to graver exploitation.

For rich and poor alike, health was precarious and married women especially suffered terribly in childbirth and by the high death rate of children. It is heart-rending to read the records in letters and diaries or even in parish registers and on tombstones. A friend of the Verney family writes 'I pray God we may add a little to the peopling this world, as well as the encreasing the Kingdom of Heaven with little angels.' Typical is the case of Lady Fanshawe who had six miscarriages and fourteen children and of these only five lived to grow up, or of a young Yorkshire woman who died aged 32 at the birth of her sixteenth child, of whom six were born dead. There are many records of third, fourth or even fifth wives. Midwifery was practised by self-taught women and it was usual for five or six neighbours to be present at the birth.

Women were still the chief doctors for all minor ailments, but it was not always safe for her to be too wise for witchcraft was firmly believed in. Indeed its persecution had increased during the seventeenth century. Earlier, witches were

21 An illustration from the 1728 edition of *The Pilgrim's Progress*. Christiana with her viol and Mercy with her lute playing for Ready-to-Halt and Much Afraid to dance together for joy at the death of Giant Despair and the destruction of Doubting Castle.

accepted as part of the scheme of things, but with the growth of Puritanism peaceful co-existence came to an end. Any visitation of sickness among people or cattle might be dangerous to poor suspected witches. Some of them might just be more intelligent than the average, some merely old and odd and a few, certainly, spiteful and unpleasant if nothing worse. Many lost their property or even their lives.

The heroic matron of the Civil War left on her own to fend for herself and her family, the fashionable frivolous new woman of the Restoration, the busy housewife, the idle gossip, the virtuous recluse, are all to be found in the great best-seller of the day—*The Pilgrim's Progress*. The second part of this famous book was written for women and especially for those who had welcomed the earlier volume—

> *Young Ladys, and young gentlewomen too,*
> *Their Cabinets, their Bosoms and their Hearts*
> *My Pilgrim has.*

This sequel is in no way inferior but it is different, gentler, more homely, with more humour and poetry, and the contrasting characters of Christiana and Mercy, so alive and moving even to-day, represent for us, perhaps more vividly than any other contemporary writings, the best of womanhood in this tumultuous age.

4 1688 to the French Revolution

The accession of two more Queens—Mary II and Anne—was not without effect on the history of Englishwomen for they set an example of sobriety which was greatly needed after the excesses of the Restoration Court. Prominent authors of the early eighteenth century, Defoe, Addison, Steele and Swift were all concerned at the decline of feminine morality and education and they tried to remedy this by writing especially for women and by articles in the new popular periodicals, *The Tatler* and *The Spectator*. This was the august beginning of the tremendous flood of magazine material aimed at women which has been pouring forth ever since. These eighteenth-century articles were essentially didactic, but they were also amusing and, as leisure was on the increase among townswomen of means, they filled a new need. They were followed by the novels of Samuel Richardson, also written with an eye to the ladies, and though he too meant to reform as well as to please, he was immensely popular.

The life of a fashionable woman then was very idle and empty-headed. It is satirized in Pope's *Rape of the Lock* where Belinda's toilet and card and tea tables are treated with mock solemnity.

> *And now, unveiled, the toilet stands displayed,*
> *Each silver vase in mystic order laid . . .*
>
> *Here files of pins extend their shining rows,*
> *Puffs, powders, patches, bibles, billet-doux.*
> *Now awful beauty puts on all its arms*
> *The fair each moment rises in her charms.*

Or there is Swift's biting *Journal of a Modern Lady (1728)*.

> *The modern dame is waked by noon,*
> *Some authors say, not quite so soon.*
> *Because, though sore against her will,*
> *She sat all night up at quadrile.*

He continues to describe her day which is filled by dress, gossip, the vapours and boredom till it is time for cards again.

The anonymous *Catechism of a Town Lady* runs thus—

> *Q. How do you employ your time now?*
> *A. I lie in Bed till noon, dress all the afternoon,*
> *Dine in the evening and play cards till midnight.*

Q. Pray, Madam, what Books do you read?
A. I read lewd Plays and Winning Romances.
Q. Who is it you love?
A. Myself.
Q. What! nobody else?
A. My page, my monkey and my lap dog.

Lord Halifax in his *Advice to a Daughter* writes 'Ladies live in a circle of Idleness, where they turn round for a whole year without the Interruption of a serious Hour.' All these and many more, testify to the depths to which the eighteenth-century gentlewoman had fallen. The newly fashionable spas of Bath, Tunbridge Wells and others played their part in this idle roundabout. Defoe wrote of Bath in 1722 'this was a resort for cripple and diseased persons, but now we may say it is a resort . . . that helps the indolent and gay to commit that worst of murders, that is to say killing of time,' and of Tunbridge Wells 'The Ladies that appear here are indeed the glory of the place, . . . company and diversion is in short their main business.' Tea, coffee and chocolate now entered women's lives for the first time, offering fresh opportunities for visiting and gossip.

22 Fashionable life towards the end of the eighteenth century.

23 Tea-drinking became fashionable, especially among ladies. Here is an English family at tea painted in 1720.

The popularity of tea as a drink for ladies was such that the tea table and all its appurtenances was symbolically assigned to the lady of the house as her special property and was left to her by the head of the family. Thus Ralph, first Earl Verney, left to his grand-daughter the tea table and silver tea kettle, lamp and stand.

Girls' education was at a terribly low ebb. Both Steele and Dr Watts remarked on the social precocity of little girls 'who can manage the tea table at ten years old', and at fourteen 'learn all the airs and graces of the world' but can scarcely thread a needle or write their own names. The curriculum at girls' schools, except for music, consisted almost entirely in dancing, deportment and useless decorative handicrafts such as paper and wax work.

It was deplorable that women should be so silly and the reformers rightly set themselves to improve their minds in order to mend their manners. But now, for the first time since Plato, the idea began to dawn in men's minds that education for women should include some sensible rules of health and hygiene. This aim of educating the whole personality came to England in the first place from France, for although throughout the century the two countries were continually at war, yet French influence had a powerful effect in English society and their philosophers, from Molière and Fénelon to Rousseau, wrote with insight and inspiration about women.

24 At the close of the eighteenth and the beginning of the nineteenth centuries the influences of Rousseau, Dr Erasmus Darwin and the Edgeworths led to some effort to improve the health of girls and women by freer clothing and more exercise. But the movement died away and did not revive again until the latter part of Victoria's reign.

It was recognised by some at least that their silliness was due 'to ignorance and lack of healthful education' rather than to their sex. Indeed at this period the townswoman was probably less healthy than ever before. She had fewer household duties to perform, took very little exercise and from an early age was squeezed into unnatural shapes by the absurd but universal fashions. In William Law's *Serious Call* Matilda is a well-bred and pious mother yet her daughters are afraid to meet her 'if they are not laced as straight as they can possibly be.' They are starved to improve their shapes and when the eldest died her bodily organs were

25 This charming picture by Chardin of a girl with a shuttlecock illustrates both the stiff and restricting clothes worn by gentlewomen in the eighteenth century and also the one active game which they were able and encouraged to play. It was occasionally prescribed by a physician to improve their too common poor health.

26 From a water-colour drawing entitled 'An Elegant Establishment for Young Ladies' by Edward Francis Burney, a nephew of Fanny Burney. It laughs at the importance laid on deportment in the upbringing of girls. The fashions are of the Empire style which came in after the French Revolution.

found to be distorted and displaced. The new periodicals had many an article on this tyranny. 'A little girl is delivered to the hands of her dancing master and with a collar round her neck the pretty wild thing is . . . forced to a particular way of holding her head, heaving her breast and moving with her whole body, and all this under pain of never having a husband if she steps or looks away.'

With such fashions healthy exercise was almost impossible. Dancing was very popular but movement was stiff and restricted. An occasional game of shuttle-cock was sometimes prescribed by enlightened physicians to be played as a duty for half an hour mornings and evenings. Walking was considered most unladylike, but riding in moderation was approved. One healthful occupation was introduced which has never lost its attraction for women right up to our own day and this also we owe in the first place to French influence. Madame de Genlis made gardening fashionable for ladies and garden plots became the latest innovation in expensive girls' schools.

As the century advanced, health and morals and rational employment made headway but the reformers made no secret of the fact that they disliked learned women. *The Spectator* scoffed at the shopkeeper's wife who had taught herself Greek 'and was too mad for Bedlam.' They preached that 'the great and indispensable duties of women are of the domestic kind. All she has to do in this world is contained in the duties of a daughter, a sister, a wife or a mother.' They are told to be 'content with a moderate share of wit, a plain dress and a modest air. Their ambition to excel will be directed to being shining ornaments to their fathers, husbands, brothers and children.' Man's idea for women has hardly changed since the Middle Ages. As for scholarship, the Tudor and early Stuart paragons might not have existed. 'If you once consider that after all the pains you may be at, you can never arrive in point of learning to the perfection of a schoolboy,' wrote Swift to Lady Betty More.

Yet, even as he wrote, a group of women appeared, as remarkable as the earlier scholars, and with so much less encouragement that they seemed to emerge on the scene as suddenly and as fully armed as the Goddess of Wisdom herself. These were the famous bluestockings called after a certain Benjamin Stillingfleet renowned for his blue stockings and his excellent conversation. The name, originally applied with honour to both sexes, soon became confined to women only and finally ended up as a term of ridicule for any female pedant. The fame of the French salons formed and presided over by a witty intelligent woman had reached England and though it never actually took root here its

27 (*left*) 'Tight-lacing, or Fashion before Ease'. From a picture by John Cotter satirizing the prevailing harmful fashions of his day.

28 (*right*) 'Dressing for the Ball', by the great caricaturist Rowlandson, shows the extravagance and vanity rife in the fashionable world of the latter half of the eighteenth century.

29 Portrait of Lady Mary Wortley Montague by Kneller (1720). She was one of the famous Bluestockings, a witty and clever woman, an intimate friend of Pope and Addison. She went to Constantinople with her ambassador husband and from there wrote entertaining letters describing the country and the people. She also wrote and published satires but is perhaps best remembered for having introduced the practice of inoculation into England.

example inspired the English bluestockings to attempt, among their own circle at least, something of a social revolution.

One of the earliest of their number was Lady Mary Wortley Montague who was also the first of that intrepid band of women travellers who have won well-earned renown. From Turkey she brought back the discovery of inoculation for smallpox which was the forerunner of vaccination. She had her own child inoculated as a proof of her conviction and persuaded Queen Caroline to follow her example.

Lady Mary's travels gave her a wider view of life than most people. 'To say the truth,' she says, 'there is no part of the world where our sex is treated with so much contempt [as England] . . . We are educated in the grossest ignorance and no art omitted to stifle our natural reason. If some few get above their nurse's instructions, our knowledge must rest concealed and be as useless to the world as gold in the mine.' Though passionately in favour of learning for girls, Lady Mary adds 'At the same time I recommend books, I neither exclude needle-work nor drawing . . . I think it as scandalous for a woman not to know how to use a needle as for a man not to know how to use a sword.'

Another interesting early bluestocking was Elizabeth Elstob. She was an authority on Anglo-Saxon, 'the first Englishwoman that ever attempted that antient and obsolete language' wrote one in her praise, continuing, (for he never dreamed of the great future company of women University graduates in English language and literature) 'and I suppose also the last.' Elizabeth was encouraged by her brother, but when he died, she was reduced to teaching village children to read and write for 4*d.* a week. She was rescued from this and became governess to the Duke of Portland's children which she and everyone else considered the height of good fortune.

30 The Ladies of Llangollen, from a contemporary drawing by Lady Leighton. The two bluestocking friends are sitting in their library. They loved poetry and gardening, kept a cow, made butter and 'spoke most modern languages'.

Such was the attitude towards scholarship for women. Conditions improved slowly and the later bluestockings—Mrs Chapone, Mrs Boscawen and Mrs Thrale—enjoyed the friendship of eminent men such as Richardson, Lord Lyttleton and Dr Johnson. They were famous hostesses whose parties followed the French pattern and who were celebrated for their good conversation. A contemporary rhyme shows how far these women had travelled from the subjects of Pope's and Swift's satires.

Let Chapone retain a place,
And the mother of her Grace
Each art of conversation knowing
High-bred, eloquent Boscawen;
Thrale, in whose expressive eyes
Sits a soul above disguise,
Skilled with wit and sense t'impart
Feelings of a generous heart . . .

Fertile-minded Montagu,
Who makes each rising wit her care
And brings her knowledge from afar!
Whilst her tuneful tongue defends
Authors dead and absent friends;
Bright in genius, pure in fame,
Herald, haste, and these proclaim!

The influence of the bluestockings was primarily social rather than, as with the Tudor paragons, scholastic and religious. They tried to rescue women from the low esteem into which they had fallen but their work had to be done all over again in the Victorian era. Although famed first and foremost for their social gifts, they were all women of great intellectual ability and among them are found the first stirrings towards the idea of a higher education for women. An early project for a Ladies College is to be found in Mary Astell's *A Serious Proposal to the Ladies for the Advancement of their True and Greatest Interest,* and this was followed by *Millenium Hall* by Sarah Scott in which an institution for the training of 'accomplished women of an honourable rank and behaviour' is described. Lady Mary Wortley Montague confessed that she would like to have been the head of a foundation for women, and two friends, Lady Eleanor Butler and the Honourable Sarah Ponsonby, made history by declaring their decision to choose learning and friendship rather than matrimony. They lived together happily for 50 years working in a library containing portraits of their bluestocking friends. They also loved gardening and were pioneers in a long line of independent, studious, energetic and contented spinsters.

To the last, however, the bluestockings retained a cautiousness where their learning was in question. One of the latest of them, Elizabeth Smith, born in 1776, who taught herself nine languages, did her best to hide her achievements

31 'The Air Pump' by Joseph Wright of Derby (died 1797). This dramatic picture of an early scientific experiment shows that women and girls were permitted to take an interest in such things though, here, the reaction of the girl, who cannot bear to watch the imprisoned bird, is perhaps more typical of girls than of boys. Public scientific lectures and experiments continued to be popular throughout the nineteenth century and were often attended by women, while it was considered unwomanly to show an interest in Latin and Greek.

32 Detail from 'Gin Lane' by Hogarth. The consumption of strong cheap spirits was one of the greatest evils especially among the poor.

and spoke of knowledge being 'the fine clothes of an upstart for a woman compared to the natural heritage of a man.' Curiously enough an interest in science was held to be more respectable for a woman than the Classics. Fanny Burney discontinued her Latin lessons with Dr Johnson for fear of becoming conspicuous but was not ashamed of going to see and to hear about Caroline Herschel's astronomical discoveries. Fanny, the first woman novelist, an art in which women have proved themselves the equal of men, wrote her earliest and most famous book in a disguised handwriting, and in spite of its enormous success feared that if it were known to have been written by her 'she would lose her reputation'. This did not happen, and novel writing became almost a respectable occupation for women, though Jane Austen covered up her writing when visitors called and the Brontës and George Eliot published under male pseudonyms.

The influence of the bluestockings was all to the good and did something to counteract a new image of women which spread through society from the mid-century onwards. This was the sentimental heroine greatly encouraged by Richardson's novels. The amount of emotional sensibility shown by his characters was the measure of their value. The term 'sentimental', in direct opposition to its use to-day, was then highly complimentary. 'Everything clever and agreeable is comprehended in that word' wrote Lady Bradshaigh to Richardson in 1749. Richardson wrote first and foremost for women and particularly appealed to the newly-emerging leisured middle-class. His heroines, full of gentleness, humility and excess of feeling influenced Rousseau and through Rousseau reached a yet wider public. The exaltation of emotions, one of the chief characteristics of romanticism, fixed a pattern for womanhood throughout the next century.

33 Education was at a very low standard for the poor both in the town and the country. Here is an illustration of the Dame who kept the village school in Crabbe's poem *The Borough*, 1810. She was both deaf and lame and probably knew little more than the alphabet.

If life for women of means began pretty badly in the eighteenth century, it was of course much worse for the poor. The death rate leapt up in the towns due to overcrowding, lack of sanitation and the prevalence of cheap gin. Hogarth's *Gin Lane* and Defoe's novel *Moll Flanders* together paint a grim enough picture of debased womanhood. Moll was a homeless girl driven inescapably to crime. Sentences upon women for trivial thefts were savage. Moll's mother was transported for stealing some pieces of linen and Moll herself was condemned to death for taking a bundle of silk. The condition of women in prison was utterly degrading and it was not until the work of Elizabeth Fry in the early nineteenth century that the situation improved.

There were efforts made in other directions to help poor women, such as the Magdalen Hospital (1758) 'to care for and rescue penitents'. Gin was at last taxed more heavily (1751) and tea became cheaper and took its place as the working woman's favourite drink, though the poor were lectured on the iniquity of spending their money on it. The death rate began to fall after the middle of the century and the standard of living for the poor improved generally. For education, the poor girl had to depend on the charity and workhouse schools. Charity schools had increased in number but deteriorated in quality. They had been started with the aim of providing something better for girls than a training solely in manual crafts and so had taught reading, writing and some arithmetic. But later, many charity schools for girls dropped all book-learning as superfluous or even harmful. As for the old system of apprenticeship, this was now often merely disguised slavery. There were laws to protect girl apprentices from the worst excesses of exploitation but they were frequently too helpless to seek legal protection.

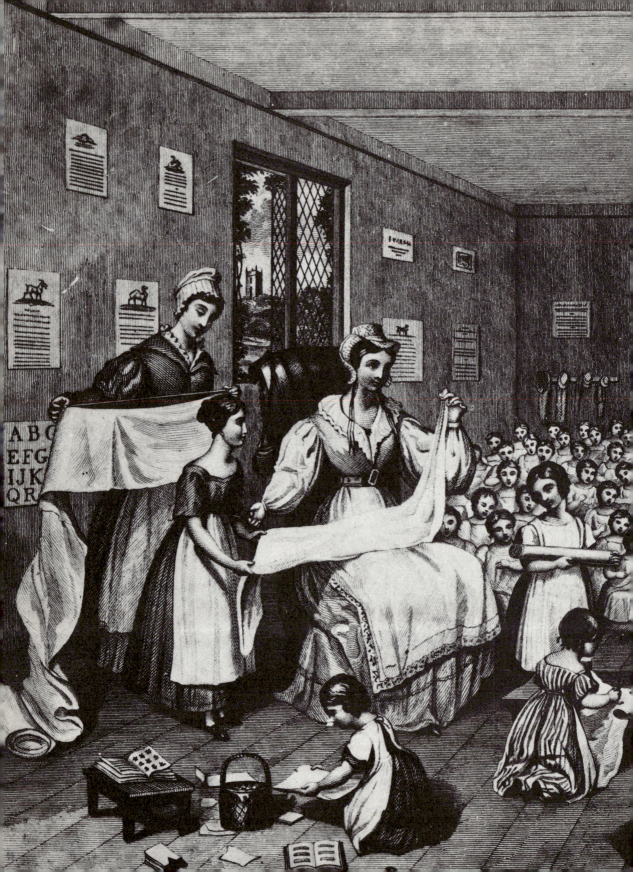

Hannah More and Mrs Trimmer, two early voluntary philanthropic lady workers, were inspired by the plight of these poor creatures. They devoted themselves to combatting the dark ignorance of the working girl and woman. Their books were printed in their thousands and influenced elementary teaching for a century. Hannah More in her youth had been a member of the bluestocking circle and the close friend of Dr Johnson and David Garrick, but in later life she withdrew from society and gave all her energies to starting schools for the poor in her home district of the Mendips and to writing very cheap educational and religious stories which led in 1799 to the formation of the Religious Tract Society. This last of the famous bluestockings left a fortune of £30,000 to charitable trusts.

There had been a slow improvement in the education, morals and general esteem of women throughout the century and, once more, invigorating ideas were beginning to cross the Channel from France, where the forces of liberty were gathering strength. But the resulting upheaval, the Napoleonic Wars and above all the enormous changes brought about by the Industrial Revolution changed the whole face of things and at first, as far as women were concerned, appreciably for the worse.

34 A charity school for girls (1810): one of the better schools where the Lady of the Manor 'stretcheth out her hand to the poor'. There are signs that reading and writing were taught here as well as needlework and it is probable that the children were given the cloth with which to make themselves aprons.

5 The Industrial Revolution—Slaves and Dolls

The English country woman had not changed much through the centuries. George Eliot gives us a wonderful portrait of her and her home in the person of Mrs Poyser. But when *Adam Bede* was written the Mrs Poysers were on the decrease. For, at the end of the eighteenth century, as a result of enclosures, of the merging of small into large farms, of the depression due to the wars with France and finally, with the invention of the spinning jenny and the power loom: according to William Cobbett 'all our properties, all our laws, all our manners, all our minds changed.' Many small farmers were ruined and the farm labourer lost his livelihood and his cottage. At the same time his wife lost the income she earned from the hitherto home industries of spinning and carding. Families were forced to migrate from the villages, in fact the New Poor Law of 1834 moved them compulsorily from the agricultural south to the manufacturing north. Disraeli, in his novel *Sybil* makes one of the native northerners exclaim: 'Ah! them's the 'himmigrants' . . . they're sold out of slavery and sent by Pickford's van into the labour market to bring down our wages.'

It was then found that the new machines could be worked more cheaply by women and children than by men. In 1834 for instance the *highest* average wage for women was 9s. 8½d. compared with 22s. 8½d. for men. The effect of wars and the emigration of young men was a surplus of single women who were

35 Mrs Gaskell, in her novels *Mary Barton* and *North and South*, draws a contrast between the country cottage home and the neglected town dwelling of the factory hand. In this picture by a little known artist, E. T. Davis, a village mother is busy giving her two children their supper.

36   Village industry carried on in the home.

forced to be self-supporting. Cheap labour was there for the asking and the proportion of women to men employed in the cotton, silk and woollen mills was round about 70:30 per cent. In 1843 in one district there were only 785 males in the factories to 5,225 females.

Enormous and far-reaching changes in the lives of working women were set in motion, at first only for the worse. Though women and girls had before often worked long hours in their own homes, at least they *were* in their homes, able to keep an eye on their families and often enjoying healthy surroundings. These cottages were now exchanged for closely-packed slums to which the women returned after working from 13 to 18 hours daily or even at night. 'The vast majority of persons employed at night and for long hours during the day are female. Their labour is cheaper and they are more easily induced to undergo severe bodily fatigue than men.' Conditions in the coal mines were far worse and here, too, women and children were employed as the cheapest form of labour.

37 Working in the mines: a woman drawing a loaded cart underground.

The break-up of family life among the workers was inevitable. Women had neither the time nor the energy nor the skills required for home-making. A moving picture of the losing battle fought by many a factory wife is given by a weaver, Joseph Corbett (1833). 'My mother worked in a manufactory from a very early age. She was clever and industrious ... she became the mother of eleven children. She was lamentably deficient in domestic knowledge. As the family increased, so anything like comfort disappeared altogether ... I have known her, after the close of a hard day's work, sit up nearly all night for several nights together washing and mending. My mother's ignorance of household duties; my father's consequent intemperance ... cold and hunger and the innumerable sufferings of my childhood, crowd upon my mind and overpower me.'

Mrs Gaskell in her grim novel *Mary Barton* confirms this state of affairs. 'I could reckon up nine men I know, as has been driven to th' public house by having wives as worked in factories; good folk too, as thought there was no harm in putting their little ones out at nurse and letting their house go all dirty.'

Gradually conditions began to improve. The cry 'No interference with liberty', invariably raised against social legislation, sounded less clearly in ears which had listened to Lord Shaftesbury's description of women's work in the mines. 'Women always did the lifting or heavy part of the work ... for females submit to work in places where no man or even lad could be got to labour in; they work in the bad roads, up to their knees in water, in a posture nearly double: they are below ground to the last hour of pregnancy.' The wrongs of the factory women, too, were pleaded by pathetic witnesses in the Sadler report. In 1842 it was forbidden to employ women underground and in 1844 came the 12-hour Act followed in 1847 by a 58-hour week.

Ruin to the country did not follow! On the contrary, trade improved and so did the workers' homes. There was even a little time and energy for education and in 1847 the first evening school for women was opened in Birmingham. The widest appeal to the public had been made by two women writers—Mrs Tonna and Mrs Gaskell. The former, in her novel *Helen Fleetwood* (1839), gave a carefully documented account of the life of a textile factory girl and she also wrote in *The Wrongs of Women* an equally detailed description of the hardships of lace-making and a screw factory. Mrs Gaskell, a far more talented writer, roused a storm of controversy by her *Mary Barton, Ruth* and *North and South*. Her informed, warm sympathy coupled with great imaginative ability made her books a power for social reform.

The effects of the Industrial Revolution on women, however, were not all bad and with the passage of time certain interesting developments began to appear. Women were now often the financial mainstay of their families. This bred independence in them though, at the same time, a new hostility emerged among men owing to industrial competition, and this is still active even today. Women also became conscious of themselves in a fresh way and began to band together in their own Friendly Societies. One husband who tried to make his wife leave a social gathering of one of these societies was met with—'I won't go home, idle devil, I have thee to keep and the bairns too and if I can't have a pint of ale

38 A pen-grinding factory.

quietly with my friends it is tiresome!' This factory wife had a stronger case than sixteenth-century Richard Hilles' Alice (see p. 12), but she had not any more legal right to any of her earnings. Even Mrs Gaskell had to accept the fact that her husband could and did pocket all her royalties. The *unmarried* factory girl, however, was enjoying for the first time a good measure of financial independence and with wages higher than the domestic servant or the dressmaker was able to escape from the tight control of parent or mistress. This freedom brought a quite new spirit of responsibility and enterprise to the better type of worker. 'The girls is the only thing what has any spirit left,' says one of the characters in Disraeli's *Sybil* after the failure of the Chartists. It was, in fact, in the factory rather than in the middle-class home that the Women's Movement was born.

In spite of bad conditions the factory girl was better off than the so-called apprentices to the dressmaking or allied trades which employed a very great number of women. In 1843 a commission gave evidence that many of these died of consumption. Overwork, poor diet and bad housing wore out the majority after only three or four years. 'There are no slaves in England, oh dear no, certainly not. It is true we make our milliners work fifteen hours a day and twenty-four upon emergencies, but then of course you know their labour is quite voluntary.' *Punch*, 1863. Vast orders for fashionable mourning to be delivered at short notice were responsible for many cases of blindness, for this was before the invention of the sewing machine. One witness stated that on the death of William IV she worked without going to bed from 4 a.m. on a Thursday till 10.30 a.m. on Sunday, standing nearly the whole of Friday and Saturday nights to keep awake. Sir James Clark, physician to Queen Victoria, declared that the 'worst regulated factory is not so destructive of health as the life of a young dressmaker' Hood's poem *The Song of a Shirt* published in the Christmas number of Punch 1843 gives the most haunting picture of these poor women

> *Stitch! Stitch! Stitch!*
> *In poverty, hunger and dirt*
> *Sewing at once with a double thread*
> *A shroud as well as a shirt.*

Yet dressmaking was preferred by many as being a more ladylike occupation Unfortunately sweated labour in shops and at home was harder to control than factory work and conditions showed little marked improvement until after the First World War.

What of the ladies for whom these poor girls slaved and who were far more self-consciously 'ladies' than ever before in history? It is a bitter paradox that during the same period that the working-class woman was subjected to extremes of physical hardship such as no man could be found to endure, the wives and daughters of the middle and upper classes were pampered and protected to excess. 'Females, from infancy to age are in a state of subjection,' declared *Th*

Juvenile Spectator of 1810, 'nor ought they to consider this a misfortune, on the contrary, it should convince them they are objects of the fondest solicitude.' But, it should have added, only if they are above a certain income group! The passage makes clear, however, that 'ladies' were simply subjected to another form of slavery than their poorer sisters and indeed the one grew out of and was dependent on the other.

The Industrial Revolution, by creating a great mass of female labour and a new wealthy commercial society emphasised idleness for women as a status symbol and the backwash of the romanticism popularised by Richardson and Rousseau had left behind an ideal of false refinement. The more doll-like and delicate, the more empty-headed and useless the better, and no mediaeval nun or heroine of chivalry was more completely protected from reality. The position was worsened by the huge army of cheap domestic labour which relieved their employers from the necessity for any domestic duties and even from the rearing of their children. These servants, especially in middle-class town families, usually worked long hours for low wages and slept and ate in unhealthy quarters.

As the century advanced a pall of prudery descended such as has never been experienced before or since. Sex for ladies was taboo and because of its undeniable connection with child-birth, this subject too was considered improper and its discussion shrouded with ignorance and sentimentality. Mrs Grundy as well as Queen Victoria reigned supreme. Yet child-bearing was the one inescapable experience common alike to rich and poor and though bad conditions kept infant mortality high among working mothers, the Victorian nurseries were filling up with monotonous regularity.

39 A *Punch* cartoon of 1863, 'The Haunted Lady or the Ghost in the Looking Glass': Madame La Modiste: 'We would not have disappointed your Ladyship at any sacrifice, and the robe is finished a merveille.' Sweated labour amongst milliners and dressmakers was particularly bad throughout the century.

As always, when a large proportion of women are silly and idle, their education will be found to be hopelessly inadequate. It is a vicious circle. The ideas inspired by the French Revolution were soon abandoned; they had never really taken root in England. The achievements of the bluestockings, as of the Tudor scholars, were totally ignored. It was once again considered most inadvisable for a woman to acquire any solid learning, in fact the standard of education sank lower than it had ever been before, for even accomplishments were more showy and worse taught. Schools were mostly patronised by the middle classes and were nearly all boarding. The majority were unhealthy and inefficient in the extreme. But it was more fashionable to employ a governess at home. Schools for girls were objected to not because of the low standard of work but because a girl of gentle birth might have the bloom of refinement impaired by mixing with those of less good breeding. This prejudice lasted right through the century, long after educational reform for girls had begun. In 1895 for instance a popular novelist wrote of her girl characters 'Their father had a very pronounced objection to schools

40   From *Punch* 1865, entitled 'What will become of the servant-gals?':
Charming Lady (showing her house to Benevolent old gentleman): 'That's where the Housemaid sleeps.'
B.O.G.: 'Dear me, you don't say so! Isn't it very damp? I see the water glistening on the walls.'
Charming Lady: 'Oh, it's not too damp for a servant!'

41 The family governess was often ill-educated herself; despised, lonely, overworked and badly paid. Such are to be found in the works of Jane Austen, Charlotte and Ann Bronte and Charlotte M. Yonge and though more fortunate and happier examples are also given, these were clearly the exception.

for girls, indeed, he had himself made an early resolution never to marry any girl who had been educated at school.'

Both in school and at home, however, the teachers were more wretchedly equipped and paid than in the preceding century because there was a greater demand for such employment, the only kind open to gentlewomen without means. Their lot was too often miserable, their qualifications pitiable. They were held in contempt by their employers and often by their pupils. Charlotte Brontë tells how the mother of one of her little charges who had said he loved her rebuked him—'What! love the governess!' and Jane Austen in *Emma* describes the profession as one which involved a 'retirement from all the pleasures of life, of rational intercourse, equal society, peace and hope to penance and mortification for ever'. The effect of this attitude and of the very poor attainments of the majority of these unfortunate women on the minds and characters of their pupils was deplorable. In any case, outstanding ability was firmly discouraged. When Mary Somerville, the astronomer, began to show a gift for mathematics, her father said 'We must put a stop to this or we shall have Mary in a strait jacket' and 'It's bad, it's bad,' said Mr Tulliver sadly, musing on his small daughter's love of books—'a woman's no business wi' being so clever; it'll turn to trouble, I doubt.' But the pattern of slaves and dolls could not be imposed indefinitely and in some of these same benighted schoolrooms girls were growing up who, in their time, were to revolutionise women's place in society.

6   The Great Breakthrough

The great breakthrough in the history of women came in the second half of the nineteenth century. The Industrial Revolution had produced on the one hand a mass of female labour exploited to its limit, and on the other an ignorant and parasitical leisured class. Each came to the rescue of the other. The wretched state of the poor appealed to those of a philanthropic turn of mind: Elizabeth Fry, Harriet Martineau, Louisa Twining, besides many unrecorded gentle-women who spent the time that could be spared from their families in unpaid, regular charitable work.

A contemporary account (1866) headed *Ladies Labour and the Poor* lists some of the work undertaken by the Ladies Sanitary Association. 'The chief aim is to help the poor to live in cleanliness and health . . . Now that the black cholera and pallid death are knocking at door how great is the good done by the labours of these ladies. They visit our sick poor, distribute soap and flannels and brooms and disinfecting fluids to those in need of them . . . They call notice to the misery and sickness caused by overcrowding and save poor girls from stitching all day long in stifling rooms. They provide a home for servants out of a place, teach mothers how to nurse and daughters how to cook and have taken during the last five seasons one thousand, three hundred and fifty eight parties of the poorest children to the Parks for fresh air and recreation.' Luckily it was considered quite respectable to practise philanthropy and incidentally this trained girls in self-discipline, took them out of their homes and gave them a desire for a better education so that they could be of greater use.

It is impossible to separate the great movements set going by and for women at this period. Campaigns for the betterment of the working woman, for a sounder and a higher education, for better pay and a wider choice of jobs, for storming the entry into the professions, for municipal and political votes, all these were interdependent. In the same way it is difficult to pick out individuals from among the splendid company of pioneers, most of whom were close friends and worked together for these different causes, which were yet the same cause. For it was women who achieved their own emancipation, though here and there a valuable champion might appear from the ranks of their fathers, husbands or brothers — a Mr Garrett, or John Stuart Mill, or Frederick Denison Maurice. There were some names, however, which shone out as *the* foremost pioneers in one or other particular sphere, such as Florence Nightingale and Elizabeth Garrett Anderson in that of nursing and medicine, Emily Davies in higher education and Barbara Bodichon and Millicent Fawcett in women's legal and political rights.

Before the mid-nineteenth century it was hardly possible to talk about professions for women with the sole exception of the stage. Actresses and singers had made a career for themselves since the Restoration, for where there could be no competition with the other sex, there was also no opposition. Writing could hardly be considered a profession for women when it had to be carried on secretly or under a male pseudonym, although the genius of Jane Austen, the Brontës, George Eliot and Mrs Gaskell could not be repressed, and as the century advanced, and papers and magazines opened their columns to women, it was possible to supplement an income by contributions. A few lady novelists indeed, who studied the popular taste (such as Anthony Trollope's mother), managed to earn quite large sums. Nursing and teaching, carried on without training and for very low pay, were despised and often degrading occupations.

Such was the situation when a girl, brought up in the most restricted fashion of the times, became, through sheer force of personality, a revolutionary force which changed not only the practice and tradition of nursing and all the public health services, but also the attitude of a whole nation towards its women. It is hard for us to realise today the influence that one woman exerted for over half a century. From Queen Victoria downwards no one could afford to disregard her. No wonder Barbara Bodichon in her petition for women's suffrage and Josephine Butler in her extremely unpopular work for the repeal of the Contagious Diseases

42 'Lady reading' by Charles Keene. This drawing conveys a sense of the serene and placid security which surrounded the life of the mid-Victorian lady of means.

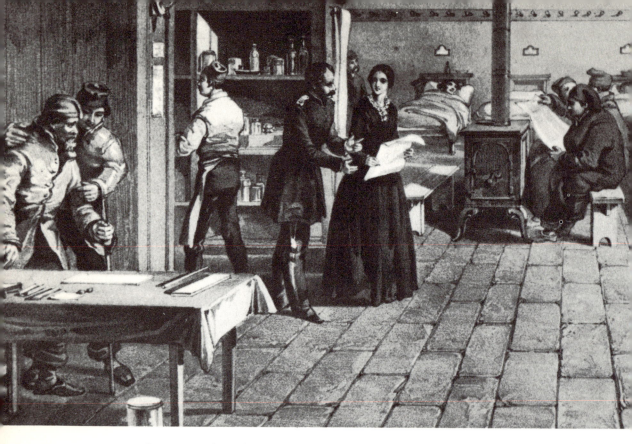

Act were triumphant at having obtained Miss Nightingale's signature. Because she belonged to the middle classes, who were the stronghold of artificial refinement, her revolt was the more telling. In a bitter early fragment of writing, *Cassandra*, she inveighs against the frustration of her sex and class—'Why have women passion, intellect, moral activity—these three—and a place in society where no one of the three can be exercised?' she cries. And again 'A woman cannot live in the light of intellect. Society forbids it. Those conventional frivolities, which are called 'her duties' forbid it. Her 'domestic duties', high sounding words, which for the most part are bad habits forbid it . . . The Family uses people, not for what they are but for what it wants them for . . . this system dooms some minds to incurable infancy, others to silent misery. Marriage is the only chance (and it is but a chance) offered to women for escape from this death and how eagerly and how ignorantly it is embraced.'

After a desperate struggle Florence Nightingale procured a nurse's training (though she had to go abroad to do so) and, when the Crimean War had made her into a national idol, she saw to it that one job at least—and that the one which has always been almost entirely dependent on women—should consist of adequately trained staff and should thus be able to claim a definite status. The Nightingale School for nurses was established in 1860. Its object was to train nurses to train other nurses. They were to take posts in hospitals and public institutions in order to raise the general standard of nursing, and it was of the

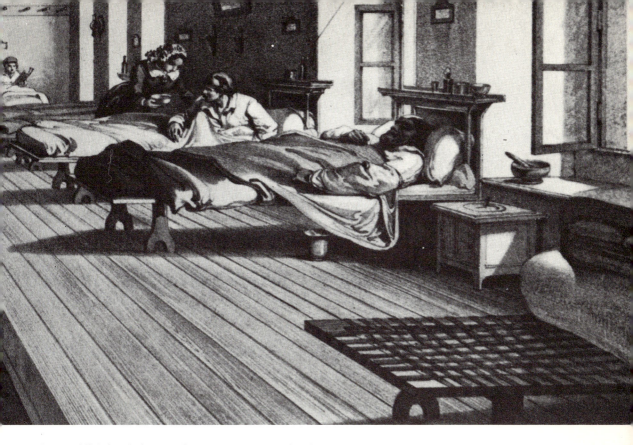

43 Florence Nightingale in one of the wards at Scutari which she has transformed into a place of cleanliness and fresh air.

greatest importance that their characters should be beyond reproach. Even this move was opposed by the medical profession who preferred that nurses should be 'in the position of house maids' as the Senior Consulting Surgeon of St Thomas's Hospital put it. It was feared that highly trained nurses might trespass on the province of doctors. This is an example of the uphill fight women had to wage to establish themselves in this most feminine of professions, even with the championship of Miss Nightingale, even at St Thomas's where her influence was strong. However, established it was, and in 1861 a training school for midwives was started with the co-operation of King's College, a move which, besides being of great benefit to mothers and babies, opened another professional door to women. Since feminine competition was feared by the Obstetrical Society, this venture was at first opposed as 'a horrible and vicious attempt on women's part deliberately to unsex themselves'.

As we have seen, from the Middle Ages onwards women had been associated with the art of healing. The most famous mediaeval hospital in Britain was at the nunnery at Sion on Thames. There was even a scheme to send women doctors

55

on the crusades. The Guild of Surgeons (1389) recognised women as members. In the seventeenth century St Bartholomew's Hospital employed women on the medical staff. Many great ladies such as Lady Falkland gave much time and thought to doctoring the poor, and in spite of witch hunts the wise woman of country districts continued to be consulted by villagers. But in the eighteenth century this tradition declined and by the Victorian age it was considered disgustingly unfeminine for women to be associated with medicine. Nowhere was this prejudice so strong as in Britain and Elizabeth Blackwell, the first English-born woman doctor, qualified in America, and set up a surgery in the New York slums for women and children. She came to England in 1859 to visit Florence Nightingale, an occasion celebrated in *Punch* by the following verses:

Young ladies all, of every clime,
Especially of Britain,
Who chiefly occupy your time
In novels or in knitting,

Whose highest skill is but to play,
Sing, dance or French to clack well,
Reflect on the example, pray,
Of excellent Miss Blackwell.

but another press comment declared 'It is impossible that a woman whose hands reek with gore can be possessed of the same nature or feelings as the generality of women.'

Elizabeth Garrett, who listened with enthusiasm to a series of lectures given by Dr Blackwell, was destined to become the first Englishwoman to qualify as a doctor and to practise in England, the first woman to take her M.D. examination in Paris, the first woman to be elected on a School Board, the founder of the first hospital to be staffed by women, the first woman dean of a medical school and the first woman mayor.

Elizabeth was lucky in her father and her husband. The one, Newson Garrett, after a short initial stage of opposition proved a convinced and powerful ally in her fight to become a doctor—the second, James Skelton Anderson, was no less staunch. But she had to fight the medical profession all the way and did so with the utmost tenacity and tact and unwearied courage in the face of constant disappointment. She got herself admitted, unofficially, to Middlesex Hospital but there was no hope of being allowed to sit for examinations and the opposition of the medical students forced the staff eventually to banish her. They drew up a memorandum which stated that 'the presence of a young female in the operating theatre is an outrage to our natural instincts and calculated to destroy those sentiments of respect and admiration with which the opposite sex is regarded.' Elizabeth, however, discovered that The Society of Apothecaries had no power under their charter to exclude her. She obtained their licence and was placed on the register in 1865. Three more women followed her example before the Society took fright and altered its charter to exclude them henceforth.

Elizabeth had to gain hospital experience by entering their reluctant doors as a nurse but once inside she found doctors to befriend her. One of these was Dr Simpson whose work on chloroform was of such great benefit to women in childbirth. After taking her M.D. in Paris, Elizabeth became a member of the B.M.A. and remained the only woman to achieve this position for 19 more years. The Elizabeth Garrett Anderson Hospital, staffed entirely by women, was founded by her and became the first women's teaching hospital. There followed a medical school for women, a scheme set going by Sophia Jex Blake and triumphantly saved from failure by the Royal Free Hospital which allowed its students to gain their experience on its staff. In 1876 a Bill was passed to enable all the licensing authorities in Great Britain and Ireland to open their examinations to women, the first to do so being Dublin, followed soon after by London University. By the nineties, owing to the patience and persistence of Elizabeth Garrett Anderson, the fiery enthusiasm of Sophia Jex Blake and the generosity of their supporters, the profession of medicine was at last open to women, though battles still remained to be fought. For instance, women were not finally admitted to the Conjoint Diploma in Medicine and Surgery before 1910. For a long time the public were not very welcoming to women doctors as a whole, but within the last twenty years or so opinion has been changing rapidly and markedly in their favour.

44 Caricature of Elizabeth Garrett Anderson, the first woman doctor in England, after she had headed the poll as the first woman member of the London School Board in 1870.

One of Dr Garrett Anderson's greatest friends was Emily Davies and it was she who remarked once to Elizabeth and her sister Millie (afterwards Mrs Fawcett) who became the first President of the Suffrage Society, 'I must devote myself to higher education, you must open the medical profession to women and you are younger than we are, Millie, so you must attend to getting the vote.' But before higher education could be thought of, girls must be helped to get a sound secondary education. That the movement towards professionalism for women sprang from their desire to be of use is well illustrated both by the career of Florence Nightingale and Elizabeth Garrett Anderson and by the history of girls' education in general.

The founding of the Governesses Benevolent Institution in 1841 was at first a purely charitable effort to assist destitute teachers of whom there were then an incredible number. But it led on to the opening of Queen's College in 1848, the aim of which was to provide some sort of accepted training and standard for the governesses of the future. Students immediately crowded into it; their standard was found to be so low that a thorough grounding in elementary subjects had to be provided besides more advanced lectures. A year later Bedford College was founded and the first steps towards establishing teaching for women on a professional basis had been taken. The demand among the pioneers was now to raise the whole standard of secondary education, the difficulties being lack of teachers, lack of capital and the general apathy or even hostility of parents. As one mother put it 'Knowing the multiplication table will be of no use to my daughter in a drawing room, so why should she bother to learn it.' But the supply of teachers was gradually improving and in 1850 the first brave venture was made by Miss Buss, at the North London Collegiate School, followed eight years later by Cheltenham College, later famous under the headship of Miss Beale. Their aim was to educate girls for sensible living and not merely to catch husbands, and to establish a good standard comparable to that required of boys.

It was in pursuit of this that Emily Davies and others began in 1863 to press for the Cambridge Local Examinations to include girls and after two years of argument, of medical reports on the physical strain involved, of opposition on the grounds that the inclusion of girls would occasion so much ridicule that no boys would deign to enter, Cambridge voted at last by 54 to 51 to extend these examinations to women. Next, in 1868, the Schools Enquiry Commission on middle-class education was persuaded to include girls' schools in its report. This was a great step forward in the assumption that girls' education was of importance to the country. The Commission found that there was still a general want of thoroughness and of system and too few trained teachers. One valuable outcome of the Commission was the founding by Mrs Grey and Miss Sheriff of the Girls' Public Day Schools Company in 1872.

Emily Davies had tried to follow up her success with the Local Examinations by persuading London University to accept women. They refused, but offered a special women's examination to which she had replied 'I am afraid that the

45 Emily Davies, founder of Girton College.

people who are interested in the education of women are a thankless crew ... They do not consider a special examination any boon at all, and will have nothing to do with it.' Elizabeth Garrett Anderson had also fought against a lower standard for the women's medical school. Miss Davies then determined to open a college of her own within reach of sympathetic tutors and professors which should offer the same university facilities as were enjoyed by men.

The scheme seemed to many a wild dream. However, in spite of the support of George Eliot, who was not considered respectable, and the opposition of Charlotte Yonge who most emphatically *was*, the project started in a very small way in 1869 with six students in a house at Hitchen near Cambridge. Miss Yonge's view was that superior women would educate themselves (though poor Ethel May in *The Daisy Chain* found little encouragement in her struggles after learning, which she pursued with the aid of her father's old spectacles and her brother's old Latin books). Undeniably, however, many clever girls did pick up the crumbs that fell from their brothers' tables. Miss Yonge also feared for the morals and health of girls herded together in schools or colleges. Her books provide valuable documentary material for the social study of the period. She is never in advance of her times, except as regards the teaching of small children, but her ideas change with the times. The early novels are strongly in favour of home education for girls, later, schools are tolerated and sometimes praised and at the last, one or two of her characters actually end up at Girton and Lady Margaret Hall.

Like Florence Nightingale's first nurses, the students at Hitchin were chosen

as much for their irreproachable characters as for their capacity. No slightest
shadow of impropriety must sully their behaviour. Even acting Shakespeare in
men's costumes among themselves was considered too daring to be countenanced.
All went well however and soon the rapidly expanding little college moved into
their new buildings at Girton. Meanwhile higher education for women was
spreading by means of local lectures in the north and a similar scheme of ladies'
lectures was started in Cambridge itself, later developing into a residential centre
which ultimately became Newnham College. By the end of the seventies London
University had opened its doors to women and Oxford had founded Lady
Margaret Hall and Somerville. The red brick universities followed suit. The
utmost economy had to be practised in the effort to provide higher education
for women. No endowments were available and women had very little money in
their own right to devote to any cause. It was a case of self-help and self-denial
for the first 50 or so years.

It was little over thirty years since the opening of Queen's College and those
years had seen established the framework of a sound secondary and higher
education for girls, not inferior to that offered to their brothers.

The movement for women's legal rights was bound up with the educational
campaign, for until women could be properly educated, their efforts could only
be fragmentary though these efforts blazed the trail. In 1792 Mary Woolstone-
craft had published her *Vindication of the Rights of Women*, a passionate outburst

46 Girls at Girton College with one of the kindly disposed Cambridge dons who consented to
tutor them.

47 Mary Wollstonecraft by John Opie. She began her career as a poor governess and later married William Godwin, the philosopher, and became the mother of Mary, Shelley's second wife. In 1791 she produced her *Vindication of the Rights of Women*, an epoch-making book, which advocated many reforms and concessions, some of which were won with difficulty in the nineteenth century and after, and some which are still being contested.

inspired by the philosophy of the French and American revolutions. She declared that women were 'a subject race' and claimed for them 'equal human rights'. In 1836 Caroline Norton (grand-daughter of Sheridan), driven to desperation by a cruel husband who was depriving her of her children, determined to get the law changed in respect to 'Infants Custody'. Married women then simply did not exist as persons, legally. They could neither sue nor be sued and could not be represented by counsel. 'I abjure all other writing till I see these laws altered' vowed Mrs Norton. She found a champion in Mr Talfourd (a friend of Charles Lamb and Wordsworth) who brought in his Infants Custody Bill which, becoming law in 1839, gave judges the power to allow injured mothers to have the custody of 'those of their children under seven'. Caroline Norton's pamphlet on the subject, (printed of course under a male pseudonym) and sent to every M.P., swayed opinion in favour of the bill, which was thought to be a great concession.

The next step forward towards attaining legal rights followed the world Anti-Slavery Convention, held in London in 1840, to which America sent four women delegates. This was held by the British representatives 'to be subversive of the principles and traditions of the country and contrary to the word of God'. The American women were rejected by a large majority and returned to work for Women's Rights in their own country. But the affair resulted in the secret growth of a similar movement in Britain. John Stuart Mill, influenced by his wife, published his *Subjection of Women* in 1869 in which he demanded women's suffrage and legal rights. 'We have had the morality of submission and that of chivalry; but the time is now come for the morality of justice,' he wrote.

But in these early days of the Women's Movement the most important of the pioneers was Barbara Leigh Smith, (later Mme Bodichon). She, like Elizabeth Garrett Anderson, owed much to a sympathetic and wealthy father who, with most unusual generosity, provided his daughters as well as his sons with an independent income. She was thus able to devote herself to those so much less fortunate—the dispossessed married women. She published a clear summary of the laws concerning women to which the Law Amendment Society paid serious attention. The outcome was a petition drafted by Miss Leigh Smith to reform the law as it affected the rights of a married woman to make wills and to bequeath her property to whom she chose. At the same time a new Divorce Bill was introduced to secure that if a woman was obliged to leave her husband she might resume possession of her own property or at least of her own earnings.

Feelings ran high. Caroline Norton declared 'This much I will do, woman though I be. I will put on record what the law for women was in England in the year of civilisation and Christianity 1855 and in the eighteenth year of the reign of a female sovereign.' The *Saturday Review* said that for married women to make wills 'set at defiance the common sense of mankind'. The first Bill was dropped in favour of the Marriage and Divorce Bill which in 1857 became law. Women might now, for the first time, divorce for cruelty or desertion though not for adultery, and the right to possess future earnings or inheritance could be given

48 Barbara Bodichon, one of the pioneers for women's suffrage.

9 Lady in the divorce court, 1870. The expression on all the faces is worth noting. Women were first allowed to divorce for cruelty and desertion in 1857.

o the injured wife. But between this date and the final triumph of the Married Women's Property Act in 1882 much hard work had to be done by Mme Bodichon nd her helpers as, even as late as 1881, the general attitude of husbands as oiced by Lord Fraser was that 'married women were already sufficiently pro- ected and why she should be allowed to have money in her pocket to deal with s she thinks fit I cannot understand.'

The philanthropists meanwhile had turned their attention to the problem of vomen's employment. *The Englishwoman's Journal*, which had been founded in 858 to voice the opinions of the new woman, printed information about employ- nent. 'It is work we ask, room to work; encouragement to work, an open field vith a fair day's wage for a fair day's work.' Miss Isa Craig, who worked for this aper, was appointed assistant secretary to the Association for the Promotion of ocial Science which became a platform for the Women's Movement. Barbara odichon founded a Ladies' Institute, a sort of club in which a strong evangelical nfluence fostered the social conscience. A society for enlarging the opportunities or work for middle-class women, other than teaching or nursing, was formed— or to tell women to get married for support was useless when there were nearly a nillion surplus women in England. A woman's employment bureau was started vith emigration schemes and classes for all sorts of trades; campaigns began to dmit women to Art Schools, and Sam Garrett, one of that invaluable Garrett mily, opened the way to law engrossing for women. The invention of the elegraph offered new opportunities to women, and female telegraphists were mployed before there was time to organise opposition. In 1880 Henry Fawcett,

63

Postmaster-General, who had married Millicent Garrett, offered girls employ-ment at the Post Office. New fields of employment contributed to the practical experience and confidence of women and so the movement towards women's suffrage steadily grew.

The first committee, with the encouragement of such men as Mill and Huxley had collected a petition signed by many famous women—among them Florence Nightingale, Harriet Martineau, Mary Somerville and Emily Davies. It was presented to Parliament in 1866 and Mill opened the first debate on the subject the following year. It was a dignified beginning to a campaign, which at first seemed to its over-optimistic supporters within sight of success. But when in 1870 the Bill was defeated, they realized that opinion must be educated to accept it. After one meeting a member of Parliament mentioned that 'two ladies, wives of members of this House, had recently disgraced themselves by speaking in public—he would not further disgrace them by mentioning their names.' One of these was Mrs Fawcett. The idea that any contact with public life was to be deplored died hard. This is once again well illustrated by Charlotte Yonge. 'I am thinking,' says one of her characters, 'whether free friction with the world may not lessen that sweetness and tender innocence and purity that make a man's home an ideal and a sanctuary—his best earthly influence. Desire of shielding that bloom from the slightest breath of contamination is . . . a great preservation to most men.' (*The Three Brides* 1876.)

None the less women were insinuating themselves gradually into positions of public authority. In 1870 Elizabeth Garrett Anderson was elected by a greater number of votes than any other candidate in the whole of London to one of the newly-formed School Boards. Since the splendid work for the reform of work-houses carried on in the mid-century by Miss Louisa Twining, a regular Work-house Visiting Society for ladies was formed which was active all over the country and in 1873 the first paid public inspector of workhouse schools—Mrs Nassau Senior—was appointed. In 1875 an Act enabling women to be Poor Law Guar-dians went through Parliament. Mary Carpenter, a schoolmaster's daughter, was another philanthropist who had not been afraid to lose her 'tender innocence' by 'friction with the world!' She opened a ragged school in Bristol and wrote papers on delinquency, giving evidence before Parliament. In 1888, when the county councils were formed, Lady Sandhurst and Miss Cobden were elected on the L.C.C. and Miss Cons was made an Alderman.

The more women philanthropists emerged from the purely private phase of charitable activities and schooled themselves to mix with men in public life, the more valuable they proved themselves in the spheres of Poor Law administration and education, the stronger became their case for municipal and parliamentary representation. The formation of women's political associations to help their husbands did much to give them experience. The Local Government Acts of 1888 and 1893 allowed women to vote in parish council elections and to hold seats on parish councils. In 1893–4 New Zealand and Australia gave the vote to

64

women and this provided fresh hope to those at home. But they were not united. The old split which had appeared in the fight for higher education and for the professions was again apparent. There were those who demanded full equality with men and those who would have been content with something less. There were even those who had worked hard in the educational campaign but who now declared that 'the emancipating process has now reached the limits fixed by the physical constitution of women'. There was also the great difficulty of finding a political party to support the cause. The Liberals were a great disappointment. They, who by their principles might have been expected to approve, were afraid that if they enfranchised women the supposed innate conservativism of the sex would turn the electorate against them. Moreover, Mr Gladstone and later Mr Asquith—the two great Liberal Prime Ministers—seem to have been personally opposed to the idea. Gladstone's view was exactly that of Miss Yonges'. 'I have too much respect', he said in 1889, 'to seek to trespass on the delicacy, the purity, the refinement, the elevation of women's nature'—to give them the vote. The Tories were more naturally unfavourable.

The National Union of Women's Suffrage, now under the leadership of Mrs Fawcett, next turned to the young Labour Party but they had other, and to their minds, more important objectives in view. For instance, they wanted universal suffrage for men without the property clause and they feared that the women's vote would interfere with this. On the whole the Women's Movement had been a middle-class campaign and though for a short time it became active in the factories and though it was a factory mill hand, Annie Keeney, who with Christabel Pankhurst, was the first to resort to militant tactics at Oldham in 1905, the cause never became really popular among the working classes. They were more concerned with representation in the trade unions.

Mrs Emma Paterson, who herself had earned her own living as a bookbinder and governess, inspired by the American Women's Union, had founded the Women's Protective and Provident League in 1875. She managed to inspire the public with some faith in the opinions of the intelligent working woman but it took twelve years hard work before the first woman factory inspector was appointed, and by this time Mrs Paterson was dead. Her work was carried on by Margaret Macdonald (wife of Ramsay Macdonald). The Women's Trade Union League grew out of the Women's Protective League, in the face of great opposition from the men's trade unions, who were afraid of undercutting. During this period the women matchmakers' strike, supported by the Women's Trade Union League and the London Trades Council, was actually successful in their demand for a living wage. (The next successful all-women's strike was that of the Ford seamstresses in 1968. It is hard to get women to strike or, once they have struck, to get them to give in.) Thus, although women's first movement towards independence can be said to have started among the factory girls at the opening of the century (as early as 1820 a Female Political Association was active among the cotton spinners), the industrial worker of later years was primarily concerned with conditions of work rather than with the suffrage.

The leaders of the movement, disillusioned with each of the political parties in turn, were now deeply divided among themselves over their future plans. One section, led by Mrs Pankhurst and her daughters, believing that nothing but extreme measures would help, turned to civil disobedience. This reached a climax in 1910 when Emily Wilding Davidson tried to stop the King's horse at the Derby, killing herself and risking the jockey's life. Violence always begets violence and the suffragettes (as Mrs Pankhurst's followers were called to distinguish them from the suffragists or moderates led by Mrs Fawcett) were imprisoned, forcibly fed when they went on hunger strike, released, and then re-arrested under the infamous Cat and Mouse Act. Many suffered greatly. Nurse Ellen Pitfield died of a wound received in a procession and left as her last declaration—'There are only two things that matter to me in the world—principle and liberty.' These women certainly showed that they were capable of losing themselves in a cause but they did both harm and good to it. Undoubtedly they alienated many sympathisers and often turned what had been a dignified campaign for justice into a sex war. Like most fanatics, in spite of their courage they were in danger of defeating their own ends. But that same courage also won them some support and one result of their notoriety was that the vast majority of those women who had worked quietly for the suffrage, and in other practical ways for women, in hospitals, schools and workhouses, were now forced to argue in support of their beliefs which had been brought into disrepute by the suffragettes. From 1906 to 1914 the country was obsessed by the suffrage question. In 1910 alone sixty new branches of the Society came into being. It is impossible to say how long Parliament would have held out had not the 1914 war changed the whole situation.

The adventurous spirit at work among all sorts and conditions of women at this time sent some exploring overseas. Two remarkable women travellers, Mary Kingsley and Gertrude Bell, not only journeyed into undiscovered territory, but set themselves to study the customs and culture of the people who lived there.

Lady Hester Stanhope had been the first Englishwoman to fall in love with the East. She crossed the deserts of Arabia and, adopting oriental dress, lived and died on Mount Lebanon. 'I have been crowned Queen of the Desert by the Dervishes,' she wrote in 1813. 'If I please, I can now go to Mecca alone. I have nothing to fear. I am the sun, the star, the pearl, the lion, the light of Heaven.' But Mary Kingsley and Gertrude Bell, through their statesmanlike knowledge of West Africa and Arabia respectively, made a greater impact on contemporary life and thought.

Mary Kingsley, born in 1862, was the niece of Charles Kingsley. She was the typical useful unmarried daughter and looked after an invalid mother and a difficult father for eight years, and, even when released by their death, she still had a weakling brother on her hands. However, 'when there were no more

66

51 Lady Hester Stanhope, 1776–1839. One of the early women travellers. She was the daughter of Lord Stanhope and the niece of William Pitt for whom she acted as hostess. After his death she left England for the Levant, settling on Mount Lebanon and adopting Eastern manners and dress. She was almost worshipped by the neighbouring tribes.

odd jobs anyone wanted me to do at home', she sailed away to find out all she could about the plants, insects, fish, animals and people of equatorial Africa.

Her great contribution, besides the valuable scientific results of her trained observation, was the discovery that the African native was not, as had been supposed, inherently evil but was a normal human being with whom friendly communication was possible. Mary was a born rebel without fear of any kind. She set herself against the authority of the government at home and the missionaries on the spot, who were engaged in breaking down tribal life without putting anything in its place that the natives could understand.

She did not, however, condemn all missionaries. She had the greatest respect for Mary Slessor, another remarkable woman, once a mill hand, who had herself acquired an impressive knowledge of and influence among the wild tribesmen of the Ohcyon district.

When Mary came home she published her most famous book, *West African Studies*, which contained much outspoken criticism of the Colonial Office. She became a national figure and was consulted by Joseph Chamberlain on matters of policy. But her advice was too revolutionary for the times. She was indulgent not only to the ordinary native, which by itself was hard enough to accept, but she also defended witch doctors, the practice of polygamy (described by her as a necessary institution supported by the native women) and though not exactly condoning cannibalism, she certainly admired the tribes that practised it! She was friendly, too, with the traders, mistrusted by missionaries and government alike. Thus many of her wise recommendations were defeated by her unpopular sympathies and in the end she felt that she had largely failed in her fight for the African natives. She died like the brave woman she always was, nursing prisoners, under terrible conditions during the Boer War.

Gertrude Bell had a happier career. Her travels in Arabia were at first in search of enjoyment and scholarship alone. She had as great an enthusiasm for archaeology as Mary Kingsley for natural history and in this pursuit she penetrated into regions where no white man, let alone a woman, had ever been before. Her journey across the central deserts of Arabia to Hayil put a line of hitherto uncharted wells on the map and cast fresh light on ancient history. Though born only four years later than Mary Kingsley, she lived on to be of great use during the First World War through her knowledge and experience of the Middle East, and she took an active part in the founding of the new Iraq State. Like Mary, she was haunted by the fear lest governments at home, knowing too little of the tribes with whom they had to deal, should take fatally wrong

52 Caricature of Gertrude Bell at an oriental party.

decisions. 'There is so much, oh so much to be thought of,' she wrote home to her father, Sir Hugh Bell, 'so many ways of going irretrievably wrong! I *do* know these people, the Arabs; I have been in contact with them in a way which is possible for no official and it is that intimacy and friendship which makes me useful here now.'

Gertrude Bell, too, died at her post but with a feeling of achievement denied to Mary Kingsley. She wrote from Baghdad, where she had lived for many years, 'I am happy in feeling that I've got the love and confidence of a whole nation.' This was overwhelmingly confirmed, not only by the testimony of the British High Commissioner, for whom she was working as Oriental Secretary at the time of her death, but from the numerous officials and representatives from all parts of Iraq and from the Arabs of the Desert.

Perhaps both she and Mary Kingsley and, later, some other women travellers, such as Freya Stark and Ursula Graham Bower, were successful in gaining the friendship of native peoples because they were not politicians, or soldiers, or traders, or hunters, but simply women, who were interested in the people they met as fellow human beings.

The period from 1850 to 1914 is of the greatest importance in the history of Englishwomen. Not only had they forced open the doors of education, of the professions, and of many fresh occupations; won a measure of civic rights and economic independence but as a result of all this the quality of the relationship between the sexes was altered for the better. The possibility of a real companionship became far more easily achieved. As the *Saturday Review,* that inveterately anti-feminist paper, put it—'a greater friendship is permitted with the other sex, there is a larger sharing of interests and women are expected to have a higher standard of education and to conceal their knowledge and culture with tasteful skill'!

That the law now recognised the married woman as an individual was significant. She could no longer be looked upon merely as an object for chivalry or convenience. One other great nineteenth-century philanthropist must be mentioned here. Mrs Josephine Butler, beautiful, wealthy, loved and loving, gave herself up to working for prostitutes. She was bitterly attacked and labelled by the Press as 'a neurotic woman with a hobby too nasty to mention'. But her firm gentleness and sincerity won many friends and supporters and in 1870 she was able to start an association whose aim was to achieve an equal moral standard for men and women and this too was a landmark.

The theme of women's emancipation in some form or other inspired many of the famous writers of the period from Shelley and the Brontës, George Eliot, the Brownings, Tennyson, Hardy, Meredith, Henry James, Ibsen, Tolstoy on to Wells and Shaw. In 1868 Mrs Punch writes to her daughter, 'Judiana', as follows: 'I cannot conceal my satisfaction that I am not writing this letter to you fifty years hence, for your dear Papa, Mr John Stuart Mill, and all reformers, prophesy such changes that the very thought of being alive then and of having daughters makes my hair stand of end. To be sure it would be a good thing for young ladies to find wholesome occupations but how overwhelming to think of one's girls being MA's and MD's and curates and Barristers and members of Parliament!' The prophets of 100 years ago were not far wrong and they certainly had grounds for optimism. The women of earlier ages had been upheld by a firm faith in the other world, the nineteenth-century women by a faith, as firm, in this one. The belief in progress animated Christian and agnostic alike and looking back over their own lives to those of their mothers and grandmothers, this faith was surely justified.

7 Two World Wars and their Effect on Women

The two wars of 1914 and 1939 brought women into national service on a wide scale so that, at last, they experienced the responsibilities, hardships and privileges of citizenship first-hand. It was lucky for Britain that women's emancipation had got as far as it had by 1914, for, in the last phase of that war, without their help in munitions, industry and agriculture, to say nothing of nursing and the auxiliary services, the country might not have pulled through.

At the outbreak of hostilities the suffrage campaign was immediately called off and many offered their services to the country. The Scottish Union of Suffrage Societies, for instance, changed themselves into the Scottish Women's Hospitals Organisation under the inspired leadership of Dr Elsie Inglis. Long before the Women's Army and Navy Services were thought of, this body raised money and personnel to equip units completely staffed by women for service abroad.

53 National Motor Volunteers Women's Reserve, October 1916, being reviewed together with their vehicles.

54 Women's Police Service during the 1914–18 war.

One was even ready within two weeks of the declaration of war, but the War Office declined their services outright. However, similar offers to the Allies were gladly accepted. Dr Inglis's record shows how the work of the early pioneers was carried on in circumstances more terrible and demanding than any they had dreamed of. She had followed in the footsteps of Dr Garrett Anderson and Sophia Jer Blake in establishing the second medical school for women in Edinburgh. Up to 1914 she had been active in the Suffrage Movement. In that year she took her hospital unit to France and then to Serbia where she and her staff are still remembered. They were captured by the Germans but managed to escape to Russia where they worked till 1917. Dr Inglis returned to England and died from exhaustion the day after reaching Newcastle.

She is only one example out of many, but the miraculous pair who were nick-named 'the heroines of Pervyse' are outstanding for sheer endurance. Mrs Knockes and Miss Chisholme originated the idea of setting up first-aid posts as close as possible to the trenches and thus saved hundreds of lives. They carried on until 1918, when they were both badly gassed. The Belgians looked upon them as almost supernatural in their courage, constancy and toughness. But a short guide issued for the use of American troops contained this general tribute— 'There is not a single record in this War of any British Woman in uniformed service quitting her post or failing in her duty under fire.' There were equally brave women, too, who opposed the war and who, in the face of fierce opposition, helped destitute German women in England, befriended conscientious objectors in prison and after the Armistice organised relief work in starving and still block-aded Germany. Foremost among these were the Quaker sisters, Joan and Ruth Fry.

73

As the war continued, more and more women, though they were not conscripted, were absorbed into work of all kinds. In 1917 Walter Long, a Conservative M.P., who had been strongly against Women's Suffrage, declared that 'the idea that women's place is the home must be met and combatted'. Can we believe our ears? Not indeed for long: for in less than two years the same women who had been welcomed or cajoled into jobs were driven back again to their homes (those that had them!) and called parasites and blacklegs if they objected. However, it was conceded that they had earned the right to a vote and the bill to give it to them was passed by so large a majority by the commons that even Lord Curzon sadly advised the Lords not to oppose it and it became law in 1918. But women under thirty were denied that vote until 1928. This odd prohibition was due to the fear that women might form a separate sex block and so outnumber the men. The National Union of Women's Suffrage Societies transformed themselves into the Union for Equal Citizenship under the leadership of Eleanor Rathbone and got to work on such problems as divorce, inheritance, guardianship of children, standards of morality, employment and rates of pay.

During the 1914 war Mrs Grundy was finally routed. At the turn of the century the invention of the bicycle did much to help. Hockey too proved a revolutionary pastime. Gymnastics had been introduced into most girls' schools by the early part of the twentieth century and compulsory games were the rule in those that modelled themselves on the boys' public schools. Though this was in some

55 Land girls in training, March 1918. This was perhaps the most crucial time of the food shortage in England due to the German submarine campaign.

56 Women tarring a road in 1918. It was due in great measure to the way women had met the challenge of the 1914 war in carrying out all kinds of work hitherto reserved for men, that votes for women at last became law in 1918.

respects a mistaken ideal, it did help to toughen girls physically and was later found to be no bad preparation for wartime rigours. But conventions were still restricting. Chaperones for young ladies were fairly common. (Their last stronghold surely was Oxford and Cambridge where they were still in use in 1920 much to the exasperation of both dons and students). Still at eighteen or thereabouts skirts came down and hair went up in a symbolic ritual.

The 1914 war swept all this into limbo. For the first time in history women were allowed to move about unimpeded and nothing could force them back into hampering clothes again, though they might choose to wear them on ceremonial occasions. In the twenties both skirts and hair became even shorter and this was significant for, after four years of slaughter, there were more surplus women than ever, most of whom had somehow to support themselves.

In 1919 Viscountess Astor was elected as the first woman Member of Parliament and the number of women returned to town and borough councils rose sharply. In the same year the Sex Disqualification Removal Act opened the legal profession in all its branches to women and resulted in the immediate appointment of women magistrates. Women were also now liable for service on juries. This Act also opened the various societies of chartered accountants to women. In 1920 Oxford admitted women to full University membership. In 1922 the Royal Society opened its doors and in 1925, after a fierce battle, the Civil Service followed suit. Meanwhile Lady Astor had been joined by Mrs Wintringham, and Margaret Bondfield became the first woman member of the Cabinet in 1929.

It is sometimes asked what difference the vote and a handful of women Members in Parliament has made. A glance at some of the laws passed and some of the campaigns set on foot during only the first ten years or so after the enfranchisement provides an answer. Twelve Acts dealing with the protection of women and children became law, and the Save the Mothers Campaign, the Infant Welfare Movement, the Nursery School Movement, the Birth Control Movement and the School Feeding Movement were all started during this period. Those who had fought for the vote had done so not merely to gain equality as citizens, but so that measures like these should be attended to. Long before, in 1911, Maude Royden, the famous nonconformist preacher, had said with reference to sweated labour and other injustices—'Such facts have made thousands of women suffragists'. From 1918 onwards, though hopes were not fully realised, yet women could feel that their special interests and grievances would no longer be ignored. Women Members of Parliament frequently received letters which began 'You being a woman yourself will understand.' But of course women's political influence is felt not only in measures affecting themselves, and the quality and importance of their contribution in Parliament has been quite

57 *(left)* Votes for Women: Cartoon by Bernard Partridge in *Punch*, January 1918.

58 *(right)* Lady Astor, first woman member of parliament, addressing a crowd during the Plymouth election of 1923. She is obviously enjoying herself answering some heckler in the crowd

out of proportion to their numbers. (The democracies of Belgium, Denmark, the Netherlands and Czechoslovakia enfranchised women during or soon after World War I. Finland and Norway had granted it earlier. The Fascist and Nazi Governments denied women the vote.)

A landmark in the social history of women between the wars was the development of the Women's Institutes. These had started in Canada as early as 1897 but the idea did not catch on in Britain until 1915 when it was at first confined to helping the war effort in growing and preserving food. But the opportunity for learning co-operation and business methods and for enlarging interests was eagerly grasped and the movement grew rapidly.

> *Is it right we should remain*
> *Shadows and housebound echoes of our men?*
> *We are homemakers; but a home's*
> *Made richer by the life that from outside*
> *We bring it—bees go foraging wide*
> *To gather sweetness for the honeycomb.*
>
> (*C. Day Lewis—Women's Institute*
> *Jubilee Book*)

59 The reviving and preserving of old crafts has been one of the activities of the Women's Institutes. Members have inspired each other to learn these satisfying skills and much fine work, especially patchwork, embroidery of all kinds and lacework has been exhibited at the Victoria and Albert Museum and elsewhere. In our machine age such outlets for self-expression are particularly valuable. Here we see a W.I. member engaged in making pillow lace.

Thousands of women have been enriched by the activities taught and encouraged by the Institutes and through them they have also concerned themselves actively in public affairs, so much so that nowadays the Government consults W.I. members on various matters and gives, in return, some financial support. The Women's Institutes have also provided a useful lesson in true democracy and have mixed up classes successfully. They have done much to improve rural life and to preserve its traditional crafts. Women are supposed to be great naggers. The Institute members have nagged to good purpose: for piped water, electric light, school buses, for a better balanced education for village children and for permission for the village nurse to use anaesthetics where necessary in childbirth. Townswomen's Guilds were later started after the same pattern.

The steady growth of women's political, rural and civic influence continued, in spite of the great depression of the inter-war years. Widespread unemployment brought its own problems and suffering to wives and mothers. They had often to bear the double burden of providing for the family and keeping the home going, while their husbands despaired of ever finding work. Sometimes, too, there was hostility to contend with for, as in all periods of surplus labour, women were cheaper to employ and so got the jobs. The 1939 war solved this particular problem though at a terrible cost. For the second time women flocked into the services and industry, but now these were organised on an even larger scale, and according to a much more carefully regulated plan. There was no longer prejudice to overcome, many were drafted abroad, and they acquitted themselves

60 The Women's Institutes and Townswomen's Guilds encourage the housewife to turn to creative work as a refreshment from the daily round of home duties. The mother who makes the opportunity to paint an entry for an art exhibition will have more in the end to give to her children.

61 Amy Johnson completed the first woman's solo flight to Australia in 1930. She had saved enough from her wages to train as a pilot but had never flown outside England before she took her frail little Moth bi-plane on this hazardous journey. For the first time she took the dangerous route over India, breaking the record to India by two days. Caught in the monsoons, she had to make a forced landing but completed the flight to Australia with a damaged wing. She died while serving as a ferry pilot during the Second World War.

as bravely as in the First World War. Almost the last Allied troops to leave Paris in 1940 were a platoon of A.T.S. telephonists who worked calmly to the last possible minute. On the Dunkirk beaches nurses were untiring—'If they have slept,' testified a wounded soldier, 'they have done so on their feet . . . we have asked them to go home in the rescue ships but each one has said "We shall go when we have finished our job." ' Later on, the Women's Auxiliary Service in Burma faced all the hardships of jungle life.

At home women helped to man anti-aircraft guns and searchlights and carried on active service of all kinds during the bombing raids. In time, all women under forty-five, unencumbered by small children, were called up for some sort of national work and those over age also often contributed as teachers, air raid wardens or in caring for evacuees. Some war-time social services carried out by women continued afterwards on a wider basis. Such was the Womens Voluntary Service which, beginning as a Civil Defence measure, now helps local authorities in all sorts of ways and receives a Government grant. Another is the Moral Welfare Association started in 1943 to look after unmarried mothers, which now employs salaried married women as workers all over the country.

Large-scale unemployment was averted after the 1939–45 war and so women were not forced back into their homes as in the twenties, though, of course, many of them were glad to return. They found many improvements to hand with

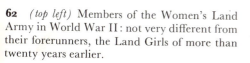

62 *(top left)* Members of the Women's Land Army in World War II: not very different from their forerunners, the Land Girls of more than twenty years earlier.

63 *(bottom left)* Girl workers painting the wings of giant bombers, December 1940. In response to the Government's appeal for increased production in aircraft, the women set to with good effect.

64 *(right)* Operating press for concrete bricks in a Welsh brickworks during the Second World War.

which they might run their houses more easily. Refrigerators, vacuum cleaners, washing machines, electric irons, cookers and heaters became commonplace, not only among the comfortably-off, but also for the working woman, while pre-cooked foods of all sorts reduced labour. Time and energy thus saved tempted many housewives to take or to retain paid work and more, though not enough, part-time jobs were made available. The new household appliances also, to some extent, compensated for the lack of domestic help for, though post-war wages were good and time-off lavish in comparison with the past, girls could not be lured into what was frequently a lonely job and one that, in England, still carried with it a social stigma. This affected the older generation of gentlewomen, who for the first time had to learn to cook and clean and look after themselves. The old stalwart army of maiden aunts, invaluable in the home and in the parish, was fast dying out. Professionally trained bachelor aunts were replacing them. In *The Philanthropist in a Changing World* Baroness Stocks has underlined the difference by an imaginary dialogue between the maiden aunt of the nineteenth century and her great-niece.

> '*What did you* do, *Great-Aunt Edith?*'
> '*I collected rents for Miss Octavia Hill. What* are *you, Great-niece Jennifer?*'
> '*I* am *a certified housing manager employed by the Barchester Diocesan Housing Trust. What did you* do, *Great-Aunt Louisa?*'
> '*I went three evenings a week to Miss Neal's Girls' Club. What* are *you, Great-niece Elizabeth?*'
> '*I* am *a club-leader under the Barchester Education Committee's Youth Service.*'

Great-aunts Edith and Louisa had also had time (with plenty of cooks and housemaids and nannies to help them) to take over whenever a crisis occurred in their own families and were often the stay of parents and of younger brothers and sisters, as well as of nephews and nieces, but full-time employed and paid great-nieces Jennifer and Elizabeth have all they can do to run their own lives.

A still more fundamental change than any yet mentioned was taking place in women's lives after the World Wars. From about 1918 onwards there had been a steady growth in the knowledge and practice of family planning. In the sixteenth century Martin Luther had written 'If a woman becomes weary or at last dead from childbearing that matters not, she is there to do it.' This remained the more or less accepted view through the centuries. As medical knowledge progressed maternal mortality decreased but continual pregnancies were still an inescapable burden for most married women. An ironically humorous view of the business is given by the Regency wit, Emily Eden—'I think it would be such a good plan if, after people have as many children as they like, they were allowed to lie in of any other article they favoured better; with the same pain and trouble of course . . . but the result to be more agreeable. A set of Walter Scott's novels, or some fine china, or in the case of poor people, fire-irons and a coal skuttle or two pieces of Irish linen. It would certainly be more amusing and more profitable.'

The new medical knowledge and the great change in social attitudes brought about a revolutionary situation in women's lives, at any rate in those of the middle and upper classes though there was great opposition and the working woman was denied help and advice for far too long. There is still much to be done in this direction for, in spite of Family Allowances (introduced by Eleanor Rathbone in 1945), the co-relation between poverty and large families is obvious. Since 1930 a voluntary organisation has set up clinics all over the country to give advice on family planning and thousands of women have benefited. Under the National Health Service only women for whom childbearing would be dangerous have been given help, but the Family Planning Act of 1967 gives the local health authorities the power—though not as yet the duty—to provide help for all who wish it. We are steadily working towards the day when no woman need have an unwanted child.

8 Today and Tomorrow

The history of the Englishwoman is not that of steady progress: the tide has ebbed and flowed. Chaucer's 'Wyf of Bath' probably found, in her own day, as much scope for love of men, business and travel as she would have done if she had lived in our century, though she might now have looked forward to a far longer life in which to enjoy herself. Had she lived in mid-Victorian times, however, the chances are that she would have been badly hampered, while a sixteenth-century yeoman's wife or a guildswoman would have shrunk in horror from the fate that most likely would have been hers at the onset of the Industrial Revolution. The sweep forward made in the last hundred years, however, is undeniable, though a few stagnant backwaters still remain, and, besides, new problems for women have arisen in our rapidly changing world.

The home has always been supposed to be the housewife's province but, in fact, she has very few legal rights allowed her. She cannot insure herself against widowhood, divorce, separation or disablement. If her husband is disabled and she has to work she cannot claim income tax relief for a housekeeper. She has no legal right to a share in the home or her husband's earnings, nor to the guardianship of her children, unless specially granted in a court of law and we have seen in a previous chapter how hardly that privilege was won. A recent report issued by the Conservative Party recommends, none too soon, that both parents should be given equal rights in the care of their children. The Labour Party's report, which was issued at the same time, advises more help for the mother who is trying to bring up her children by herself, whether she is a widow or living separately from their father. Both reports are aiming at greater legal and financial equality between the sexes. For instance, there are very few women now serving on our juries. This is because few women have the necessary property qualifications. This should certainly be altered. Again, a mother cannot give her own nationality to her children even if she is separated from her husband and living with them in her own country. A child should have the same rights with regard to his mother's nationality as to his father's, when these are different, and should choose one or other when he is grown up. The recommendations in these two reports are not firm promises but they are important as showing that both parties are thinking seriously about legal and financial equality for women in the future.

According to surveys lately made in Great Britain, Germany and France, the average working hours of the housewife per week are round about 80 (varying according to the size of the family). For these she receives no pay and is often dependent on her husband for all personal expenditure as well as for household money. There are practical difficulties in the way of payment such as who should be the pay master but these ought to be faced and the housewife's job put on a proper basis and no longer regarded (in Katharine Whitehorn's words) as 'a mixture between a holy vocation and a prison sentence'. Perhaps when economic independence is the rule for the housewife fewer married women will be tempted to take jobs outside the home.

If it happens that the father is the better home-maker and the mother the better professional or businessman, why should they not exchange the traditional roles without loss of dignity or independence? Sweden is a pioneer in this direction. There is actually a ban on books which distinguish between occupations for men and for women and in all schools, all children, regardless of sex, must take courses in domestic science, childcare and needlework. As a result the professions of nursing and child care are attracting an increasing number of men. Sweden has also introduced equal pay for women, who are encouraged to take up jobs previously reserved for men. One result of this is that it has been found necessary to abrogate some laws such as restrictions on night work which were originally passed to protect women and make it possible for them to look after their families while working. If men are willing to take equal responsibility for the home there is obviously less need for these laws and if women receive equal pay they must be prepared to do equal work at all hours of the night and day. If, too, in our own Welfare State they are in future to receive equal social benefits, they must pay equal insurance contributions, always given of course the fact of equal pay.

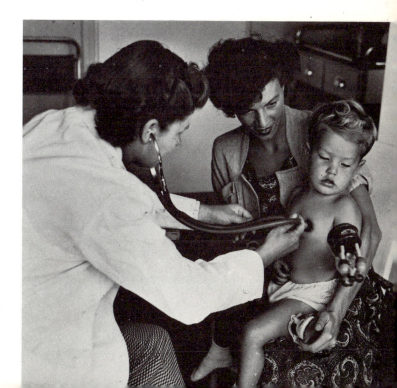

65 A woman doctor examining a child at a National Health Centre.

66 Mrs Elizabeth Lane, Britain's first woman High Court Judge.

At present about one-third of the working population of England is made up of women and of these the great majority are earning only just over half the rate paid to men. They have, besides, a limited choice of jobs and fewer facilities for training. This is partly their own fault for, as their history shows, they must rely mainly on themselves to carry through any widespread reforms and, although the Trade Union Congress has paid lip service to the principle of equal pay ever since 1888, their women members have not been active enough in pressing for it and no Government will easily give up such a productive source of cheap labour. Why have women workers not made themselves felt more? Many are too busy doing their double jobs in home and factory to spare the time and energy for political protests and many, too, are working more to escape loneliness or, supported mainly by husbands, to earn money for extras rather than for their livelihood and so they do not bother about equal pay. They also do not demand training for the better jobs in sufficient numbers, partly because they shrink from adding to their responsibilities, partly because they may even prefer routine jobs, and partly, though to how great a degree it is hard to judge, because the accepted attitudes of parents, teachers and employers are unfavourable. There is no evidence that girls are behind boys at the 'O' level stage but many after that seem to lose ambition.

In the professions and in business the pattern is roughly the same. All doors except those of the Anglican and Roman Catholic priesthood and the Stock

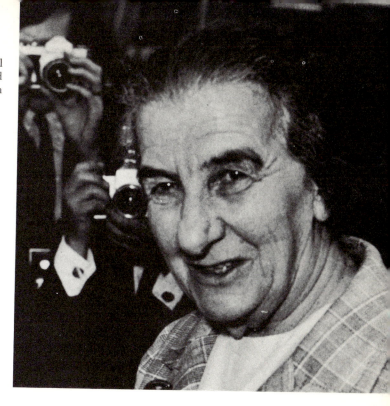

67 Mrs Golda Meir, Prime Minister of Israel – the second woman prime minister in the world and probably the most influential woman political figure at the present time.

Exchange are now open to women but except in teaching, nursing and some other social services their numbers are small and those in the top positions smaller still. The Robbins Report (1967) stated that only 8% of girls compared with 22% of boys were receiving higher education. Women in Russia and America make up respectively 42% and 37% of the student population. In England they are only 24%. This is due in part to discrimination against them which does still exist, for instance, in some medical schools and apprenticeship courses, and besides, there are too few places for women students especially in the older universities. In science and technology the numbers are far too small. This has been put down to lack of ability but in Russia women engineers make up 33% of the total engineering force so that the fact that they are very few in this country is more likely due to poor educational chances than to any sex difference.

The two greatest obstacles in the way of equality of opportunity, pay, and esteem for women, are the attitudes left over from the past and the drop-out of industry and the professions due to marriage and children. Time, it is hoped, will dispose of the first: prejudice and injustice are disappearing in the face of pressure brought to bear by organisations such as the National Council of Women, The World Association of Women Executives, the National Council for the Single Woman and her Dependants, and others. The example of other countries such as Sweden also helps. The second difficulty, that of children especially, is more complicated. It is of no use to pretend that mothers and children do not need each other and that homes are not vitally important. Family planning has reduced the average time spent by women in child-bearing to a quarter of what it took in Victorian days, but the actual rearing of a family is, because of the lack of help, in some ways more of a problem. Gone are the useful unmarried sisters and cousins and aunts, gone are all the nannies (except for the very wealthy) and the little nurse girls. No one is left but the grannies and in the modern blocks of dwellings there is often no room even for them. The labour-saving kitchen, though welcome, cannot keep an eye on the children.

Yet every year more wives take jobs and a new factor has appeared: for the first time there are now more men than women in the population. The reason for this is that more boys are born than girls and whereas, in the past, more boy babies died (the idea that women are the delicate sex is a myth, it is the other way round) nowadays medical skill keeps them alive. This means that as practically no woman need remain unmarried unless from choice, the number of wives at work will rise yet higher. How are these to be helped to fulfil themselves both inside and outside their homes and families? There should be far more part-time work available and refresher and training courses for the older woman who has left work while rearing her children. There should be many more and better day nurseries and nursery schools. The position at present about these could hardly be worse. In 1945 there were about one thousand four hundred state nursery schools; in 1968 only four hundred of these remained open. There should be easier shopping hours. Above all there should be shared responsibility for home and children. A Government Survey of Women's Employment lately revealed that two in six husbands did not even give a hand with the washing-up. There should also be a reform of the present system of taxation whereby a married woman's earnings are not taxed separately but are added to her husband's. This would help the more highly qualified professional wife to pay for assistance in her home so that she could remain in work after marriage.

Dame Kathleen Lonsdale, F.R.S., the first woman President of the British Association, quoted in her address Lydia Becket, one of the nineteenth-century pioneers, as saying that more differences were observable between women and women than between women and men. This of course is true and it is important not to forget it. Yet it is true, too, that there are certain broad psychological differences between the sexes which it may be useful to recognise. Women, perhaps because of their biological function, are generally more concerned with people than with things. They tend even to personalise the things they use in daily life. Factory girls, for instance, will talk to their machines and decorate them with ribbons. The majority of girls, if given the chance, will choose careers in which they will deal with people such as nursing, teaching and social work of all kinds. In an increasingly technological world where human beings are in danger of becoming more like ants or bees this concern with people as persons takes on a new value.

Another marked difference seems to be that women are less aggressive and violent. For every thirty men now in prison in this country, there is only one woman, and delinquent boys greatly outnumber the girls. But if women are more passive and law-abiding, this too has its dangers. Both passivity and aggression have been unhealthily exaggerated in the past because society has been a one-sided affair in which men have dominated. The achievement of a true equal partnership between men and women should result in a more balanced, creative and happier community.

1387 Chaucer's *Canterbury Tales*

1516 Sir Thomas More's *Utopia* (in which he advocates co-education)

1466–1536 Erasmus lived—one of the early champions of women

1558–1603 Reign of Queen Elizabeth I

1642–49 The Civil War

1675 *Dido and Æneas*, the opera written by Purcell for performance at a girls' school

1684 Second part of *The Pilgrim's Progress*, written for women.

1709–12 Publication of *The Tatler* and *The Spectator* aimed at pleasing and educating women

1718 Lady Mary Wortley Montague, an early 'Bluestocking', introduces inoculation into England

1740 Publication of *Pamela* by Samuel Richardson

1790 *The Rights of Women* by Mary Wollstonecraft

1813 Elizabeth Fry visits Newgate Prison for the first time

1833 First efficient Factory Act

1836 The Case of Caroline Norton

1847 The Ten Hours' Bill

1848 *Mary Barton* by Mrs Gaskell

1848 Opening of Queen's College

1849 Dr Elizabeth Blackwell graduated in medicine in NY State, USA

1854 Florence Nightingale goes to the Crimea

1857 Women allowed divorce for cruelty and desertion

1865 Elizabeth Garrett Anderson medically qualified at the Society of Apothecaries

1869 *The Subjection of Women* by John Stuart Mill
Girton College founded

1870 Women admitted to serve on first School Boards

1874 Girls Public Day School Company founded

1888 First women elected on LCC

1907 First open-air suffrage rally held in Hyde Park

1914 Outbreak of the First World War

1915 Women's Institutes founded in Britain to help the War Effort

1918 Women's Suffrage Bill passed

1919 Removal of Sex Qualification Bill passed

1919 Viscountess Astor elected as first woman member of Parliament

1919 First women police

1928 Women's suffrage extended to give the vote at twenty-one

1929 Margaret Bondfield appointed to the Cabinet
1930 First Family Planning Clinic started
1930 Amy Johnson carries out a solo flight to Australia
1939 Outbreak of the Second World War
1945 Family allowances introduced by Eleanor Rathbone
1962 Mrs Elizabeth Lane became the first woman judge in Britain
1966 Mrs Gandhi became Prime Minister of India
1969 Lloyds opened to women
1969 Mrs Meir became Prime Minister of Israel

Suggested Further Reading

Prologue and *Wyf of Bath's Tale* in Chaucer's *Canterbury Tales*, Nevill Coghill's modernised version (Penguin)
English Girlhood at School, Dorothy Gardiner (OUP)
Life of Queen Elizabeth I, Elizabeth Jenkins (Gollancz)
Letters of Lady Dorothy Osborne ed. Moore Smith (Everyman)
Letters of Lady Mary Wortley Montague ed. Brimley Johnson (Everyman)
Mary Barton, Mrs Gaskell (Everyman paperback)
Life of Florence Nightingale, Cecil Woodham-Smith (Fontana)
Elizabeth Garrett Anderson, Jo Manton (Methuen)
Mary Kingsley, Cecil Howard (Hutchinson)
Letters of Gertrude Bell ed. Lady Bell (Penguin)
Rapiers and Battleaxes, Josephine Kamm (Allen and Unwin)
Women in Revolt, J. Kazantzis (Jonathan Cape: Jackdaw No. 49)
Women and Society from Victorian Times, Gladys M. Cuddeford (Hamish Hamilton)
Votes for Women, Roger Fulford (Faber and Faber)
Women at Westminster, Pamela Brookes (Peter Davies)

Index

The numerals in **heavy type** refer to the figure numbers of the illustrations.

95